DARK POOL SECRETS

LEARN HOW TO PROFIT FROM WALL STREET'S HIDDEN TRADES THAT MOVE THE MARKET!

by Stefanie Kammerman

Cover design: Command G Design

Interior layout and design: Jeffective Design + Illustration

Printed in the United States of America

First Edition

ISBN: 978-0-692-11191-8

To all the men who told me I shouldn't and couldn't do it
To the men who told me I could, and I should
To the women who have inspired me
To all the women I wish to inspire
To my angels up in heaven
To all the angels down here on earth
I thank you
You have taken away insecurity, anxiety, and doubt
You have replaced it with motivation, courage, and desire
And for that I am eternally grateful

Stefanie Kammerman

Table of Contents

Chapter 1

HOW I BECAME THE STOCK WHISPERER

It all started the moment I was born. My grandmother Rosie, a sassy, way-before-her-time lady, bought me one share of IBM stock. As I got older, that one share intrigued me. I owned a small part of International Business Machines Corp. It made me feel important. I cared about IBM. I followed the price action every week by looking up the stock quotes in the newspaper. I got excited when it went up a point and a quarter, and I got sad when it went down a half a point. I kept track of every upward and downward movement, charting the movements in my head. Luckily for me, IBM went up most of the time. Not only did it go up, but it split quite a few times over the past four decades. If my grandmother hadn't bought me that one share of IBM, I probably never would have become intrigued with the market at such an early age, or perhaps, never at all.

It wasn't until after I graduated college that my interest in the markets shifted into a career choice. For the record, I didn't major in economics or attend business school at Florida Atlantic University (FAU). I chose to major in psychology. I was always intrigued by human behavior, but I realized after four years of studying it, I had no real desire to become a clinical psychologist. To be honest, I had no idea what I wanted to be when I graduated. One thing was certain, I had a big fat pile of college loans and I really needed a full-time job so I could pay off my loans.

None of my friends really knew what we wanted to be when we graduated. Many of us just grabbed whatever we could find. One of my closest friends, Dalya, had gotten a temporary job working for Schonfeld Securities, the largest and most prestigious proprietary trading services firm in New York at that time. Dalya was filling in as a receptionist over the summer. She had become friends with many of the traders in the so-called "million-dollar room" at the firm. She was invited to their happy hours on Friday afternoons but didn't want to be the only female, so she picked up the phone and called me. She said, "Hey Stef, would you like to join me and a bunch of guys that make millions of dollars a year for happy hour?" She added that they were really cool guys and begged me to go. She didn't have to twist my arm too much. Are you kidding me? "Of course, I'll come," I told her. There was no way I would let her down. I had visuals of these guys strutting into the bar wearing Armani suits and Gucci loafers, but when I spotted Dalya standing next to a bunch of guys wearing jeans and sneakers, I was pleasantly surprised.

I immediately started talking to Scotty, who was one of the best traders in the room. He humbly told me that he had a momentous year, making a little over a million dollars but confessed that he must have left $100,000 on the table because he had a tough time keeping track of what he was buying and selling. He expressed to me that he really needed an assistant and asked me if I knew anybody that would want to work for him. I wanted to help Scotty out, so I told him that I could be his assistant. I had to admit to him, however, that I had no experience in trading. He told me that wouldn't be a problem, that it was easy, and that he would teach me. He asked me if I could start as early as that next Monday, and I agreed that I could. This, ladies and gentlemen, was how my life changed. It was this moment that my career path was chosen.

I was never more excited in my life to start a new job than I was that Monday morning. I was a blank canvas ready for Picasso's fine brushes and vibrant colors. That first day was in June of 1994. It was a typical hot summer day in Long Island. Keep in mind that I didn't own a computer at this time. It caught me by surprise when Scotty asked me, "Do you do windows?" I looked around the room and noticed there were a lot of windows in the office.

All I could think was that he wanted me to clean all the windows in the office. When he saw my eyes widen in disbelief and fear, he quickly said, "Don't worry Stef, I'll teach you Microsoft."

Shonfeld Securities, 2 Jericho Plaza, New York

What a relief that was! Microsoft Windows had recently come out, but I was clueless. I had a lot to learn. I was ready, willing, and able.

Most people think that trading is all about money. That's what I thought too. Scotty quickly taught me that first day that trading had nothing to do with money. He was up $20,000 in the first 20 minutes after the market was open. I was so excited for him and thought he was going to break out in a happy dance, but that wasn't the case. His mood changed quickly. He started to get very upset. First, he pounded his fist on his desk as he cursed underneath his breath. I sat there silently holding my breath, not understanding why he was so upset. Next, he got up and flung his chair across the room. This wasn't the happy go lucky guy I met at happy hour on Friday. I wanted to understand what was happening, so after a minute or so, I finally gained the courage to ask him why he was so upset. He was up $20,000 dollars! Why wasn't he doing the happy dance around the room?

Scotty told me, "It's not about the money. Trading has nothing to do with the money." He told me that he lost his discipline on one of his trades. He should have gotten out of Intel (**INTC**) but he didn't. Even though he made money on the trade, he didn't follow his rules. He knew the next time he didn't follow his rules, he could get crushed. He was very upset with himself, not with the market. It was at that moment I realized I needed to learn all of Scotty's trading rules. I didn't want him throwing any more chairs around the room. I needed him to stay disciplined.

That afternoon, Scotty wrote out all his trading rules on a piece of paper for me. I was really surprised at the simplicity of his trading system. It was much easier than most would think. We were doing overnight momentum swing trading, entering our positions near the close of the day, and then exiting out of them the next morning. Scotty would find stocks that were positive, up on the first day on above average volume. This was his biggest secret and it worked. Volume was key. He told me volume was the gasoline that stocks needed to move up and down the hill. Heavy volume was heavy interest, and we were looking for our stocks to gap the next day in our favor. He was always hedged overnight. He took long and short positions. He always had cash on the side just in case. He would tell me, "never extend yourself on margin or else you may get a margin call."

We were trading in fractions back in the '90s. Scotty told me that if the price was three quarters off the high on our long swing trades, we needed to get out. Take your profit and run.

Vice versa, if the price was three quarters off the low on our shorts, we need to cover them and get out. These were stocks that usually gapped a few dollars overnight. I told Scotty that I could help him keep track of his positions. I would definitely make sure he got out when they are three quarters off the highs and lows. That's exactly what I did for the next two years. I kept track of all of Scotty's positions, making sure he entered and exited out properly, never thinking about the money. That was the only thing I focused on. That is how I learned how to trade.

I soaked up everything I could about trading. I was sitting in the million-dollar room at the biggest prop firm on Long Island. Most people would pay money to sit where I sat. Instead, I was being paid to learn from the best traders in the firm.

Does it get any better than this? Yes, it does. They sat me in front of a machine called an Instinet machine. This was the mega trading computer. The Instinet machine was a green glowing Dark Pool execution machine. You could see where all the big boys were buying and selling. Only the big firms had access to this, and there I was, sitting in front of it, doing all the orders on it for our trading table.

With this computer, you could see the **Dark Pools** of liquidity. This is how I learned about the Dark Pool. The Dark Pools are alternative exchanges where the biggest trades are being executed. If one of the traders called across the table for me to sell a specific stock, I would punch it up on the Instinet machine to see if there were buyers. If I spotted a huge buyer I would tell that trader not to sell and vice versa. This machine and my specific call outs saved my traders thousands of dollars a year.

Come Christmas time, Scotty handed me the biggest check I had ever seen in my life, saying "thank you so much for saving me thousands of dollars this year." I almost fainted when I looked at the check. It was the biggest check I had ever seen, and it was made out to me. It was a $20,000 Christmas bonus check. Even though my first thought was to run to Bloomingdales and go on a wild shopping spree, I decided it was much better to pay off all my debt, including my college loans. I knew this was just a taste of what was to come. I knew I would have plenty of time to go shopping later.

Shonfeld Securities didn't want their traders leaving for lunch. They preferred that their traders sat at their desk and traded all day long, raking in profits. In order that we could continue trading, they came up with a genius idea. Free lunch! Every morning we would fill out a lunch ticket. While we were eating our free lunch, we would watch Dan Dorfman on CNBC. He would always call out a hot stock to buy right now. We would watch as that stock would rally up sharply only to fail and come crashing back down again. We followed that pattern and started to short it every time it spiked up. This was our favorite lunch time trade. Nothing beat a free lunch and a great trade.

There were two kinds of traders at Shonfeld Securities – traders who traded their own money, and traders who traded firm money. Scotty traded his own money. This gave him a huge advantage in being able to choose which firm to trade. Traders who traded their own money could barter over commission costs. Back in the '90s, commissions were much higher than where they are at today. We were paying $19.95 a trade. Scotty did 30-60 trades a day, so it added up and became a high expense. It behooved him to try to get lower commissions any way he could. After speaking with some other firms, he found one who offered him his own trading room and much lower commissions. When he found this new firm, we transferred to On-Site Trading, Inc. in Great Neck, NY. It was very common for traders to switch back and forth among firms.

On-Site Trading, Inc. was run by two great guys – Howard Jahre and Gary Mednick. Howard was a lawyer and was responsible for watching everybody's P&L's (profit and loss). Gary did everything else. On-Site Trading occupied several floors. Scotty and I had our own private room on one of the floors. On-Site Trading supplied us with all the computers, including an Instinet, news services, and all the scanners that we needed. We made a lot of new friends at this firm. Everything was going great until Scotty announced one morning that he was moving out of New York. He told me that he was sick of paying high state taxes in New York. On-Site Trading was opening an office in Florida, and he was going to move down there. I couldn't believe that I had found my dream job… and now my boss was leaving the state. What was I going to do now?

I had just gotten married, and there was no way my husband was moving to Florida. I didn't know what I was going to do, but I didn't have to wonder for too long. I was immediately called down to Howard's office. Howard made me an offer I couldn't refuse. He offered me money to trade. He offered me $250,000. He told me I would not be responsible for the money. He would, however cut me off if my account went down $50,000. He told me that I was the first female trader to whom they lent money. He told me that he was confident in me because I was trained by the best. At that time, I didn't have enough money to trade on my own. Up to this point, I hadn't even considered becoming a trader. I was content being Scotty's assistant. This was life changing for me.

We had about eight traders in my room. Frank sat to my left and traded his own money. His motto was 'Slow and steady wins the race.' To the right of me was Anthony who traded the firm's money. Anthony worked for the airlines at night and was trying to switch careers and make money as a trader. Alex sat diagonally across from me. We called him the "Crazy Russian." He was a very aggressive trader but a great addition to our room. These guys were like brothers to me. I trained many of the new guys that came into our room. I quickly learned that training as many traders as I could was a huge benefit to our whole room. It always came back ten-fold. These new traders would call out great trades. I taught them exactly what to look for, and they found them for all of us. Teamwork at its best.

I never thought about the money, just like Scotty taught me. I only focused on following the rules. He would always say, "If you don't think about the money, the money will come." He was right. My first year as a trader for On-Site Trading, I did extremely well, even after paying commissions and interest.

I was nicknamed "**The Trading Goddess**", being that I was the only female trader at that time. However, I never felt any different than the guys. I didn't even notice I was the only female until our annual Christmas party. We weren't allowed to invite our spouses, so there I was, the only female surrounded by about a hundred very drunk male traders. That was when reality set in. I realized that I was the only woman. By the time Monday rolled around, however, I was just a trader again.

Every year they had a special reward for the trader of the year at the firm. They would announce the winner at the Christmas party. That first year, Frank and I won the Rookie Trader of the Year award. They handed us both a $250 gift certificate for Peter Lugers Steak House, and Howard offered me another $250,000 with which to trade … that was the best gift of them all.

I traded for the next year or so until I became very pregnant with my daughter Michelle. I started to have Braxton Hicks contractions and needed to go on bed rest. I'll never forget my delivery. There I was at North Shore Hospital, Wednesday, August 12, in the throes of childbirth. CNBC was playing in the background, and my gynecologist, Dr. Victor Klein, was giving me stock quotes off his new state-of-the-art watch. He was obsessed with the stock Computer Associates (**CA**) at the time. You could say I was just a little obsessed with the stock market when I chose my daughters initials to be MRK after Merck & Co., Inc. (**MRK**).

I was very fortunate from the gains that I had made trading that I could stay at home with my daughter and not have to go back to work. I'll be honest with you. As much as I loved being a full-time mom, I really missed my career as a trader. I really missed the market. I would have loved to trade from home, but keep in mind this was 1998. We were still on dial up. My internet was not fast enough, and I didn't have all the great software that I had at On-Site Trading. Not being able to see where the Dark Pool was buying or selling left me at a huge disadvantage. I decided that I would do some longer-term trading and help my friends and family by giving them a heads up on what stocks I thought were going to move. Every time I went to a party, people would come up to me and ask me for stock tips. I started to have a reputation in my small community of being **The Stock Whisperer**. I would make my recommendations based on volume and price action. Two of my first recommendations were Microsoft (**MSFT**) and a then relatively new company called America Online (**AOL**). When those stocks made huge moves, my friends were hooked. They wanted more.

I almost went back to trading full time when my daughter Michelle was a year old. I revisited my old firm and will never forget what happened. This young kid came running down the hall when he saw me coming. He gave me this huge bear hug and thanked me profusely. I remembered training him a while back. I taught him our special overnight momentum trading system. He was an awesome student. He followed every single one of my rules. He excitedly told me that he made a million dollars that year because of everything I taught him. I was blown away by his success. I did very well, but I didn't hit the million dollar a year mark when I was there. I was so proud of him and so honored that I had helped him achieve success. It was at that moment that I desired to go back to work. That night I told my husband that I wanted to go back to my old firm and start trading again. The next morning, I found out I was pregnant again with my second child, Max. I guess I wasn't going back to work yet. Even though I didn't go back to my firm, I continued to do longer term trading from home with much success. My goal was to double our IRA account while raising our kids.

Raising two kids two years apart was quite challenging, but I loved every single minute of it. I loved attending every single parent/teacher conference. I especially loved being the parent picked to go on school field trips. One of my favorite memories was when Max's kindergarten teacher, Ms. Lupardo, walked into this lake wearing galoshes trying to catch a fish. The expressions on these kids' faces were priceless. My son and I still laugh about this years later.

In 2009, my kids were 9 and 11 years old. I realized that technology had come a long way and that I could trade from home effectively. I had found software that would give me all the Dark Pool trades, giving me a huge edge. I knew that following the big boys was the best way for me to trade.

I joined an online trading room and started calling out my trades in the room. After making so many great calls every single day, the other traders begged for me to do a class so that I could teach them what I was doing. Over the next four years, I put together various workshops which sold out immediately. I was asked to run the online trading room and jumped at the opportunity. It reminded me of my old trading table back in the '90s. I knew that if I could train all 250 traders in this room, they would call out amazing trades all day long and that's exactly what happened. Our room was on fire, and we were all profiting from it. I was being paid only a very nominal amount to run the room. I felt that I should have been earning a lot more for all the work I was doing. I'll never forget the day I asked for a raise. I was watching CNBC and they did a whole segment on why women don't get paid the same amount that men do. The answer was that women didn't ask for it. I remember picking up the phone and calling my boss to ask for a raise. I was all pumped up after watching that segment. I just knew that all I had to do was ask.

What happened next may surprise all of you, because it certainly surprised me. I got fired. I was in shock that this plan didn't work. I got over it fast. I am a big believer that everything happens for a reason. All the traders in the room were so upset that I was leaving. I felt so horrible for them. They depended on my knowledge and my guidance every day. This was their career. This was the way that they put food on their families' tables. I was coaching them every single day, in real time, calling out high probability trades, helping them enter and exit trades. Suddenly that was coming to an end. I knew I had to come up with a plan to help them. So I did.

I decided to start my own online trading room, The Java Pit. After all, this was something I had been wanting to do for some time. This would, however, take a few months to set up. I told my traders to be patient. In the meantime, I was going to create accounts on Twitter and StockTwits to post up all the Dark Pool trades. I didn't want them to miss anything. I continued to trade and call trades out on social media. These traders were like my family, and I had to help them.

What I didn't realize was that I was creating a trading log, and that I would eventually have thousands of followers. I couldn't believe how many people didn't know about the Dark Pool. I didn't realize how many people were trading out there that needed to be educated. This was when I realized that this was my calling: to help as many traders out there that I could. Since 2013, I've been on three tours with Larry Berman across Canada. He is one of the biggest portfolio managers in Canada and has a show on BNN every Monday called "Berman's Call." I have also been on tour with the MoneyShow and TradersEXPO as one of their premier speakers. I've been traveling across the country speaking to various trader meetup groups. I've been on television and on the radio teaching as many people as I can about the Dark Pool.

Over the last 24 years I have seen first-hand that the market is rigged. In fact, it's highly manipulated. The purpose of this book is to shine a light on the Dark Pools and teach you how to profit from these machinations.

Chapter 2

DIVING INTO THE "DARK POOLS"

Dark Pools existed long before my early days on the Instinet machine at Shonfeld Securities. Dark pools have been around since the beginning of time. It used to be called the upstairs room, and only the elite had access to it. Over the years, the Dark Pool has significantly grown in size, and increasingly more investment firms are trying to gain access to it. Over 40 percent of the total volume traded in the stock market is being executed in the Dark Pool. This is huge! This is almost half of the total volume, and these are the guys that are in control of the market.

As a trader, you look for any advantage to make money. Working with Scotty, we found an edge trading against the market makers who had to make a market for a specific stock. The market makers were all lined up on the level 2 quote with the price and the amount of share size they wanted to buy and sell of the stock. Our advantage was gained by following the dominant market maker.

Most of the time, the dominant market maker was Goldman Sachs. Goldman dominated most markets by buying and selling the most shares. You never wanted to go up against the big guy so if Goldman was on the bid with a huge order to buy the stock, traders would follow their lead and buy the stock. If Goldman was buying in huge size, that stock was going to go up. Likewise, if Goldman was on the offer with a huge order to sell the stock, most of us traders knew not to buy it. In fact, if we were already in that stock, we would sell it knowing that Goldman wanted to sell a large order. Being able to see where Goldman was buying and selling was extremely helpful and profitable while trading. Goldman eventually realized that all the traders were watching their orders as it became increasingly more difficult for their orders to get filled.

Goldman got smart. They started hiding their orders on alternative exchanges where they could be anonymous. One of those alternative exchanges could be accessed using the Instinet machine. This was the first computerized execution platform for the Dark Pool.

Below is a picture of what the level 2 used to look like back in the 1990's. At the time, the market was trading in fractions. Circled in the center column of the image, Goldman Sachs (GSCO) was looking to sell 1000 shares on the offer of SUN Microsystems @ 91 11/16. Also, circled in the left column is an order on the bid to buy 5500 shares @ 91 1/2. That is the anonymous order, but we can make an educated guess that Goldman is the market maker. The order was being put out through the Instinet Dark Pool exchange (INCA). Ironically, this anonymous order is the largest order on the Level 2 quote.

In today's market, the Dark Pool is a series of networks that allow traders to buy and sell large blocks of shares without running the risk that other traders will see their hands. How does Goldman Sachs sell 20 million shares without moving the market down? They don't have to report one single share being sold until their entire order of 20 million shares is filled. It's not enough that these large traders are given an edge not afforded to retail traders, but they are also given up to three hours to report their trade to the trade reporting facility (TRF) that trickles down to the consolidated tape.

These trades aren't being executed on the NYSE or the Nasdaq exchanges. They're being executed on alternative trading systems (ATS). An ATS is not regulated as an exchange since they are typically registered as a broker-dealer. Trading through an ATS works in the favor of large institutional investors because of the lack of transparency and anonymity. Large blocks of shares are filled electronically and are often times executed between the bid and offer. When you're trading huge size, every penny makes a huge difference.

Currently there are over 40 ATSs, or Dark Pools, registered with the SEC and are classified as either broker-dealer owned, exchange-owned or electronic market makers. The two most popular broker-dealer owned Dark Pools are Barclays' Liquidity Cross (LX) and Goldman Sachs' Sigma X. These two platforms have been getting a lot of attention lately, and let's just say it hasn't been good attention. They have been fined for unscrupulous activities in their Dark Pools.

Barclays and Credit Suisse are fined over US 'dark pools'

⏱ 1 February 2016 | Business   ≺ Share

Barclays and Credit Suisse have been fined a total of $154m (£108m) by US regulators for their US "dark pool" trading operations.

On February 1, 2016, Barclays was fined $154 Million for letting high frequency traders front run in their Dark Pool. High frequency traders aren't even supposed to be trading in Dark Pools. It's illegal. Barclays not only let them in, they let them front run all the orders. These fines were just a message, not a punishment. Compared to the profits that Barclays made, $154 Million is insignificant.

Goldman Sachs also got into some trouble with their Dark Pool, the Sigma X.

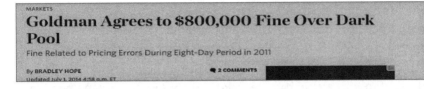

MARKETS

Goldman Agrees to $800,000 Fine Over Dark Pool

Fine Related to Pricing Errors During Eight-Day Period in 2011

By BRADLEY HOPE   2 COMMENTS
Updated July 1, 2014 4:58 p.m. ET

On July 1, 2014, Goldman Sachs was fined $800K for price discrepancies in their Dark Pool. More than 395K transactions executed in Sigma X were executed far away from where the stocks were trading. In other words, these were bad fills. Again, this wasn't a punishment. Goldman Sachs makes more than $800K before you and I even have our breakfast in the morning.

On November 1, 2016, Goldman Sachs hired Nasdaq to run its Sigma X Dark Pool. The news stated that Goldman will now be outsourcing day-to-day operations of its Dark Pool following an industrywide regulatory crackdown. Nasdaq will be providing the underlying technology and additional surveillance for Goldman Sachs' market.

Even with all of the illegal activities and manipulations, we can profit off of them if we know how to spot them. This is what I will be teaching you. This is what I've taught thousands of traders over the past two decades. This is how we spot rallies and corrections before they happen. We can see when the big boys are buying or selling by following the Dark Pool prints. From gold and silver to oil, natural gas, copper and steel, banks, bonds, the US dollar, high tech, social media, you name it: it all starts with the Dark Pool. For my traders, this is the holy grail of trading.

I don't pay for special research, nor do I get any phone calls from the "higher ups". I don't need any of that. All we need are the prints. We can easily see the prints from the guys that pay for special research and get those phone calls. In order to capitalize on these large prints, you need to understand the tools and data available for peering into the Dark Pools.

On June 2, 2014 FINRA began to make Dark Pool data available. This data was already available to investors and professionals on a real-time basis through securities information processors (SIPs), but the trades weren't attributable to a specific Dark Pool. FINRA's new transparency initiative has now made the data available, free of charge, to the non-professional investing public on their website. While it's nice to get as much information as you can get, the timeliness of the information is critical. Through FINRA you can get data for Tier 1 NMS stocks on a two-week delayed basis, and all other NMS stocks are released another two weeks following that. How's that for transparency!

There are many people out there that will tell you that you can't see the Dark Pool trades in real-time. They believe that they are invisible. The problem is that they aren't using the right software. Their software doesn't have a Dark Pool data feed. That's why they can't see it. There are only a few brokers out there that have it. I use most of them. I believe it's always good to have as much back up as you can. It's not a usual occurrence, but it does happen, that one platform may have issues for the day. I can't trade without the Dark Pool, so besides using Charles Schwab's StreetSmart Edge˚, I also use Lightspeed™, DatatraderPro.com, and LIVEVOL˚ Pro.

Charles Schwab's StreetSmart Edge˚ trading platform has an amazing indicator called the Block Trade Indicator. This indicator allows you to display large quantity trades based on the minimum block size you want to see. Not only are the blocks coming from the exchanges, but it also includes Dark Pool data. Watching this indicator, you can see large orders filled at prices that seem to be outside the current market prices. This may just be a delayed Dark Pool print that I'll cover later in the book. I use this indicator for all of my real time Dark Pool prints.

The second tool is the CBOE LIVEVOL˚ Pro trading platform.

The platform was originally designed for professional option traders but has expanded their line-up for retail traders as well. LIVEVOL˙ Pro has historical time and sales data that goes back several years and it also includes any Dark Pool prints. This is the tool that I use for my historical Dark Pool prints.

This is how we can find the highest probability trade set-ups. The best way I can teach you about this is to show you actual pictures of these Dark Pool prints along with how my traders and I mapped out our trades and executed them in our live trading room.

> *I had been trading fairly successfully since 1995. That all changed in 2014 when I met Stefanie. We met on accident as I was in Vegas to see an acquaintance in a live trading competition. His opponent was Stef. I was immediately drawn to some of the items she talked about during the competition, so much so that I decided to take in her presentation later in the day. It turned out to be one of the best decisions I have ever made. I joined her room the following week and never looked back.*
>
> *Chad S. Czappa*
> *Tower Capital Investments, LLC*

Chapter 3

COUNTING THE CARDS OF WALL STREET

My mother, Roberta Birdt, was a highly intelligent master bridge player. Her secret was that she knew how to count cards. She ran the biggest bridge game in Florida, teaching thousands of people how to play over many years. I asked her once if it was easy to teach people how to count cards. She told me that it was very easy to teach, but that one had to practice it to truly master it.

What happens to professional gamblers who can count cards in casinos? They get kicked out, right? The casino always wants the best odds, and card counters don't fit in with that plan. I will be teaching you how to count the cards of Wall Street. The good news is that they can't kick us out of our casino, the stock market.

Counting the cards of Wall Street is old fashioned tape reading. I wanted to learn as much as I could about trading, so that very first day on the job at Schonfeld, I asked Scotty what book I should start with. He didn't hesitate for a split second before he spoke. He told me hands down, to read **Reminiscences of a Stock Operator** by Edwin LeFevre.

I ran out after work to Barnes and Noble and bought the book. I stayed up all night long reading it. I couldn't put it down. I was absorbing every single word. I spent the night highlighting my favorite quotes, and by the end of the night, my book was quite colorful. This book was good. This book would become my trading Bible.

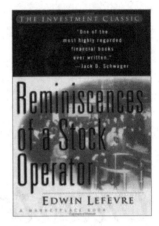

What impressed me most about this book was that although it was originally published in 1923, nothing has changed. Everything that applied to the market and to trading then is still relevant today. Edwin LeFevre interviewed Jesse Livermore for a few weeks, and this book was the outcome.

Jesse used to get kicked out of the old bucket shops for reading the tape. Can you imagine if your broker closed your account tomorrow because you were able to read the tape and you were making too much money? That is exactly what happened to Jesse Livermore. He read the tape, made lots of money, and kept getting kicked out of the bucket shops. The bucket shops had pictures of him on the wall as if he was a criminal on the most wanted list.

Jesse Livermore's life and his trading rules have made a significant impact on my personal approach to "reading the tape." As a result, I want to share with you a couple of my favorite quotes from the book.

The first quote from Jesse is all about timing:

"Everything happened as I had foreseen. I was dead right and I had lost every cent I had!"

Why do analysts make the worst traders? My guess is because the market never does what it's supposed to do when it's supposed to do it. The market doesn't make any rational sense. It's all about supply and demand. It moves up when the big boys are buying it. It moves down when the big boys are selling it. Once you learn how to read the tape, you'll never have to think again, which leads me to my next quote.

"I do not allow my possessions or my prepossessions either to do any thinking for me. That is why I repeat that I never argue with the tape."

The tape never lies. You should always stay on the right side of the tape, and I'll be showing you many examples throughout the book of how this is done. As you can see, great traders have been reading the tape for a long time.

The tape today is our time and sales window. How many of you watch your time and sales window while you're trading? If you said yes to this question, you are on the right path. For those of you who said no, I hope that by the time you have finished reading this book, you will see just how important it is that you do so for your success as a trader. It's an easy tool to add onto your screen. Most trading platforms provide real-time time and sales data.

There are **four different types** of **Dark Pool prints:**
1. Real-time prints
2. Late buy prints
3. Late sell prints
4. Market on Close prints (MOC)

I will be showing you examples of real-time prints and late buy prints in this chapter, but will cover late sell prints in Chapter 9 on *How to Spot a Correction Before it Happens*. Market on Close prints are just institutions getting out of positions that were held overnight and aren't meaningful to us.

Real Time Prints

Let's start with the real-time Dark Pool prints. These trades are happening right now. We know this because the price of the print is where the stock is trading at that exact time. These are simply large orders that will have a large bias on the price action. In other words, this stock is going to have a huge move very soon. I always visualize a rocket about to take off when I see very large prints. Let me show you an example on Facebook (**FB**).

On July 27, 2017, we spotted the biggest print on Facebook that we had ever seen. This happened right after Facebook's earnings came out. I don't ever try to peg the top. How many of you have ever tried to peg the top on a huge move up? It's a great feeling to sell at the top, or short at the top. I learned how to go short very early on because Scotty was a big bear. He loved to short the market, making money on the way down. He would say, "They take the stairway up, and they take the elevator down." There is fast money to be made on the short side when the market is having a correction, or a stock is having a correction. This was the case with **FB** that day.

The stock had run up $8.44 after it had a big earnings beat.

Below is a picture of the daily chart taken from my DAS Trader Pro platform. I've drawn an arrow to show you the gap up.

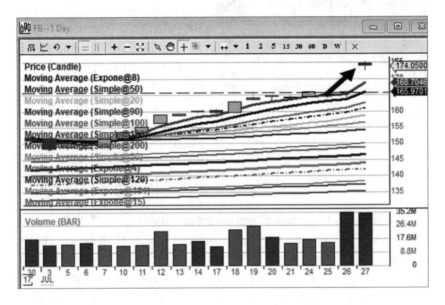

I was able to find this print using StreetSmart Edge®'s block trade indicator. Since Schwab has a Dark Pool data feed, I use this to scan the entire market for all the big trades. I set my scanner up in four columns. The first column is for all trades that are 50K in share sizes and higher. The second column is for all trades that are 500K and higher. The third column tracks the major index ETFs and what I refer to as fear indicators. The fear indicators are the VIX-related ETFs. I call this column my correction indicator. The last column focuses on gold, silver, steel, oil, natural gas, copper, and the dollar. Many of us in the Java Pit trade these commodity-related stocks and ETFs.

Block Trade	Link ◇ ⤢ _ ▢	

| 500K | SPY | pre | Banks | + |

| II Pause | Actions ▼ |

Symbol	Trade Price	Trade Size
FB	174.60	3607000
SIRI	5.86	500000
CHK	4.90	500000
CMCSA	39.96	650000
CHK	4.90	750000
JD	46.05	840000
SIRI	5.84	735900
QQQ	145.82	513000

In the picture you can see where I highlighted the large **FB** print that I spotted in my 500K column. We spotted a 3.6 million share print on **FB** at $174.60. That's almost a $630 Million trade. I want to try to peg the top only if Mark Zuckerberg is selling.

So many traders over the years have asked me if I pay attention to **unusual options activity** (UOA). UOAs often cause the option prices to rise just on increasing implied volatility (IV). I feel it's best to pay the most attention to the underlying asset, the stock prints. You want to catch those option chains off guard. You want to buy those options cheap. The only way to do that is to see the unusual Dark Pool prints on the stock. This is exactly what happened on **FB**.

When we spot a huge unusual print on a stock or ETF, I'll tweet it out immediately. Below is my tweet on **FB**.

Thestockwhisperer 🔒 @darkpoolwhisper · 20h
Massive $FB print, is that you Zuckerberg? 3.6 mil $174.60 Bullish above 175 Bearish below 174

I map out the trade for all my followers in all my tweets. I help them by calling out the levels to be bullish above and bearish below. In this case we were bullish above $175 and bearish below $174. How do we know if it's smart money buying or selling Facebook? This is what I tell my traders: visualize throwing a huge rock into the lake. It's going to have a big splash. You want to give it some good room around the print. If **FB** were to break above $175, we would assume it was smart money buying and go long buying the stock or buying some call options. If **FB** were to break below $174, we would assume it was smart money selling and we would go short, selling the stock or buying put options. You'll hear me say this a lot, **Bullish above, bearish below, no thinking!**

Now is a good time to take you inside my live trading room. My traders come from all over the world. Here is a map of the locations of my traders that day on July 27.

Traders were logged in from Morocco, Spain, France, Germany, the UK, the US, Mexico, and across Canada. Even though we come from all over, we all share the same passion for trading. It's an amazing community of beginner, intermediate, and advanced traders. We trade stocks, options, futures, Forex, and cryptocurrencies. It doesn't matter what you trade, it's all about following the Dark Pool in our trading room.

I've trained my traders to call out the unusual prints and oh boy, do they. At 11:35am Keith, aka Keke, called out that **FB** had a 3.6 million print. Look at the chat thread below:

11:35	**Keke**: 174.60 3.6 mil	
11:35	**Wall St Wiz**: lol AMZN too over confident for its earnings? GOOGL v2.0 today?	
11:35	**Blanca P**: BABA testing print	
11:35	**Amit M**: massive FB print!	
11:35	**Amit M**: 3.6 mil 175	
11:36	**Keke**: Mark Zuckerberg selling lol	
11:36	**Amit M**: Stef, wathc refreshing here ... and exit if sellers are coming in	
11:37	**Ricki B**: andif so, then exit	
11:38	**Wall St Wiz**: wholly FB 174.60 3.6 million	

Another great trader in our room, Amit, aka Bam Bam as well as the Crypto King, said it must be Mark Zuckerberg selling.

A few minutes later, we spotted another 3.6 million share print on **FB**. Whenever we see something like that, it's usually a price change of the first print. Let me show you what that looks like on my LIVEVOL˚ Pro software.

The trade at 11:32am was canceled and replaced by a different trade at 11:45am. You can see the same share size, but the price was changed from $174.5981 to $174.2833. While we see real-time Dark Pool prints at any time during the day, we find that trades that happen right around lunchtime are best.

Late Buy Prints

How do we know when a correction is over? We see late Dark Pool buy prints on the **SPY**.

The Dark Pool is buying and hiding their orders from us. Everybody thinks that Trump winning the presidential election sparked the rally in the market.

I am going to show you that the big guys were buying in the Dark Pool, before the election, on November 4, 2016. That's how they were able to hide their trades from us until the next day.

We see this pattern after every correction. When I see this, I tweet it out immediately. On November 7th, I tweeted that I had seen late Dark Pool buy prints on the **SPY** from Friday at $208.48. Whenever we see this, we are always bullish above. The smart money was buying and hiding it at $208.48. As long as we remain above this level, we will be bullish. Below is my tweet:

They are like cockroaches. When we see a few of these, there are always more. At 3:52pm I tweeted that we got a lot more of these late Dark Pools buy prints.

We ended up getting another 9 million late Dark Pool buy prints on the **SPY**, all at $208.48. They kept printing all day long. Let me show you a picture of them:

Time ▲	Symbol	Qty	Price
11:56:49	SPY	1003418	208.4822
12:00:16	SPY	501718	208.4822
12:01:30	SPY	501709	208.4822
12:05:17	SPY	1003418	208.4822
13:14:53	SPY	501759	208.4822
14:29:01	SPY	501759	208.4822
14:40:27	SPY	501718	208.4822
14:45:12	SPY	501759	208.4822
15:23:38	SPY	501759	208.4822
15:30:12	SPY	501759	208.4822
15:41:52	SPY	501718	208.4822
15:49:12	SPY	501759	208.4822
15:50:40	SPY	501759	208.4822
15:52:32	SPY	501759	208.4822
15:54:01	SPY	900000	212.4500
15:54:10	SPY	501759	208.4822
15:54:10	SPY	501759	208.4822
16:00:00	SPY	3313694	213.1500
16:00:00	SPY	3313694	213.1500

11/07/2016
Hi: 213.19
Lo: 211.3
O : 211.45
C : 213.15
V : 109,794,861
211.021
AVG:211.288
AVG:214.616
AVG:212.690
AVG:215.340
AVG:214.444
AVG:210.487
AVG:208.415
AVG:207.139
AVG:213.668
AVG:210.996
AVG:213.562
AVG:211.498
AVG:212.076

Here is the Open, High, Low, Close (OHLC) from November 7, 2016 for the SPY:

You can see the low of the day is $211.30, and the **SPY** never traded at $208.48. This is a very bullish sign.

You can see the SPY went up quite a bit after that, and it didn't matter who won the Presidential election. The Dark Pool was buying. Instead of calling it the Trump rally, it could have been called the Clinton rally, if Hillary won.

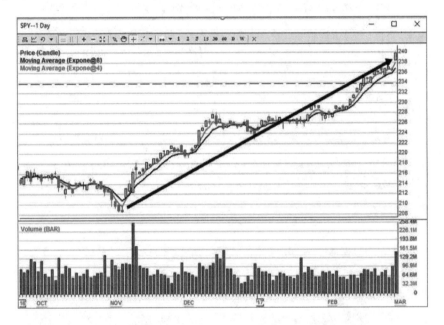

In the Java Pit, being an educational trading room, I am continually teaching traders how to trade. I help my traders in the Java Pit by calling out when stocks are hitting specific levels. I'll call out entries and exits as well. I am a huge believer that the best way to teach people how to trade is to teach them during live market hours.

"Stefanie Kammerman is the most friendly, approachable, and experienced trading coach we have ever had. My wife and I have been in other trading rooms that charge WAY too much money and have very subjective rules for their trading plan. Stef is different – she is definitive with her rules – and her rules bring results. Results that feel calculated and expected – not accidental or lucky.

Stef specializes in following the smart money, specifically big Dark Pool prints. She says first comes the prints, then comes the news, then comes the move – prints always come first. She teaches you how to read the prints and what to do about it.

For example, on June 7, 2017, we made a trade in BABA before the close of the day because there was a huge Dark Pool print. The next morning we closed it out and made over 1966% ROI on the trade! THAT is real results.

Of course, we wished we would have met Stef a long time ago, but we are with her now and have never been happier."

Thanks for everything, Stef!
Bruce Linker and Laura Geres

Chapter 4

BULLISH ABOVE, BEARISH BELOW

Everybody wants to know my secrets. How do I continuously find the right stocks every single day? How do I find these specific levels? I don't just tell my followers to buy a specific stock or short a specific stock. There is always a level.

Some traders use technical indicators such as Wyckoff patterns, volume spread analysis, Elliott waves, and Fibonacci retracements and extensions. Some use MACD, RSI, stochastics, and other indicators. While these may be helpful, all these indicators are lagging indicators. The only one that is the first signal, not lagging, is prints. **PRINTS.** The prints always come first. Follow the smart money. Watch and follow the Dark Pool.

Many people miss a lot of the underlying commitment of Dark Pool traders when just looking at the price chart and indicators. Maybe they see little movement in the price on light volume. Inevitably they're missing what is really happening behind the scenes.

The real volume may be happening off the exchange in the Dark Pool. Seeing a large Dark Pool print tells you that there is a high degree of commitment to take the stock in a direction but based on the print you won't know if the stock is being bought or sold. This is why the level is so significant. If the price moves above the print, it tells you that the commitment is to take the price higher. If the price moves below the print, it tells you that the commitment is to take the price lower. **Bullish above, bearish below, no thinking!** I showed you a glimpse into how I specify levels in the previous chapter on the **FB** trade.

Often times these big directional trades happen after the price is moving indecisively. Traders call these moves a "breakout." Sometimes the indecision lasts less than a day and at other times it can go on for weeks. The first step is to identify a significant Dark Pool print to find the level. The next step is to trade a direction based on the movement. In this chapter I'm going to teach you how to trade the print during consolidation phases, and during intraday consolidations phases using candle patterns.

Consolidation Phases

One of the ways indecision manifests, is when the price is consolidating. The price is consolidating when the price trades within a well-defined range followed by directional moves up or down. I only trade a stock when I see the Dark Pool trading it, and the Dark Pool loves to enter a trade during a consolidation phase.

There are two types of Consolidations:

1. Accumulation = Buying
2. Distribution = Selling

Look at this daily chart of **PYPL** in May of 2017:

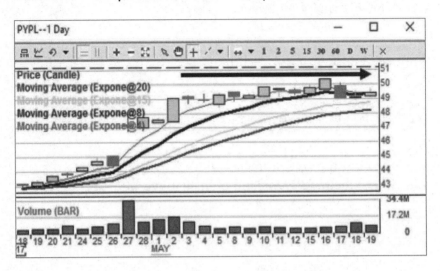

As you can see, **PYPL** had been consolidating throughout the month of May. Consolidation can easily be spotted because the stock is going sideways. Stocks don't go sideways forever. At some point, the consolidation period ends, and the stock will move. The million-dollar question is: Are the big boys buying here or selling here? Was it accumulation? Or was it distribution?

It just so happens we started to spot some very interesting prints coming in on **PYPL** on May 22. Here is the transcript from my trading room from that day:

Nitro called it out first. He noticed the 998K print on **PYPL** at $49.60.

10:44 **Nitro**: PYPL print 998k @ 49.60

I noticed another one at 12:17pm.

12:17 **Stefanie Kammerman**: PYPL print
12:17 **Stefanie Kammerman**: 49.74 800k

I mapped out the trade for the room. At 1:10pm, I wrote that I was bearish below $49.50, and bullish above $49.75.

13:10 **Stefanie Kammerman**: Bearish below 49.50 PYPL bullish above 49.75

Look at the 15-minute chart of **PYPL** from that day:

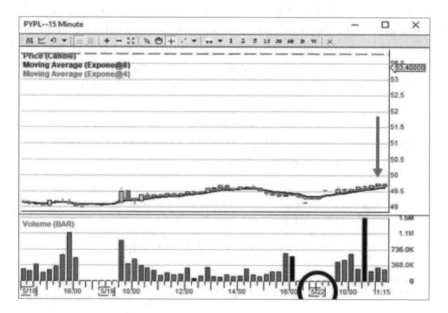

At 2pm, I announced that I bought **PYPL** because it was above the prints.

[14:00] **Stefanie Kammerman**: B PYPL above prints

Many of my traders also took the trade as well. I covered up their last names here for privacy.

15:24 **Bob**: gonna swing PYPL calls

15:26 **Georgia**: Swinging PYPL calls too

15:59 **Verminator**: bot PYPL calls

The stock closed strong, on above average volume. Look at the chart where I have circled the volume. **PYPL** also closed above the 8 EMA, another bullish sign.

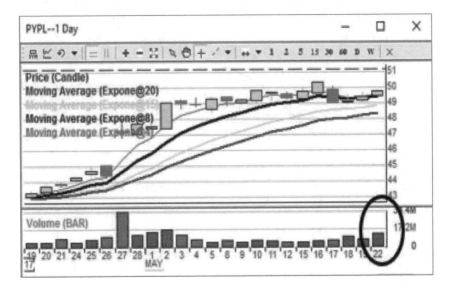

Here is a screenshot of all the big prints that day:

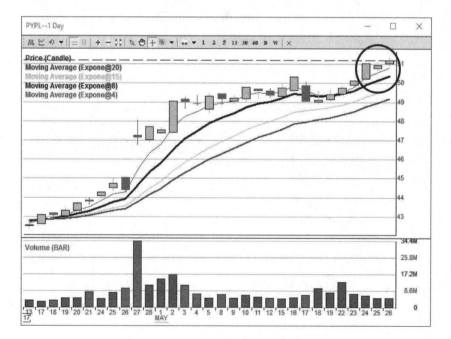

Time ▲	Symbol	Qty	Price	Exchange	Condition	Market
10:43:57	PYPL	998050	49.6000	NQNX	IntermarketSweep	49.64 x 49.65
12:17:25	PYPL	880000	49.7350	NQNX	Canceled/Regular	49.73 x 49.74
13:05:34	PYPL	880000	49.6300	NQNX	Derivative	49.55 x 49.56
13:05:34	PYPL	880000	49.6300	NQNX	Derivative	49.55 x 49.56
13:28:52	PYPL	2000000	49.6500	NQNX	Regular	49.64 x 49.65

I liked it so much I put it in my **Whisper of the Day** video the next morning.

The Stock Whisperer @VolumePrintcess · May 23
Today's #HOT #Whisper $GM $XLF $MGM $PYPL $FCX $GDX $UGAZ $USO

Do you want to guess what **PYPL** did next?

PYPL went up over the next few days to $51. My traders did very well on this trade.

10:01   **Verminator**: out 1/3 PYPL calls +30%

10:04   **Stefanie Kammerman**: stopped out of half PYPL +.55

11:43   **Di**: out PYPL 50 call +40%

While we took some profits, many of us added onto our positions as well.

14:17   **Verminator**: adding to PYPL

On May 25, we spotted something very peculiar... late buy prints at $49.47. I tweeted it out immediately:

Thestockwhisperer @darkpoolwhisper · May 25
Late Dark Pool Buy prints $49.47 $PYPL bullish above 51

We see late buy prints from time to time using the Block Trade Indicator. Sometimes, we see prints on Schwab's Dark Pool feed that we don't see in other Dark Pool feeds.

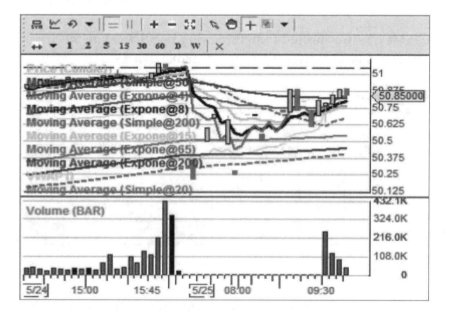

Block Trade	Link ◇ 🗗 _ ☐ ✕
500K	SPY pre Banks +
‖ Pause	**Actions ▼**

Symbol	Trade Price	Trade Size
PERI	1.50	2699400
PYPL	49.47	500000
PYPL	49.47	500000
PYPL	49.47	500000
CMCSA	40.41	4156600
F	10.95	482367
CMRE	7.05	543983
RSX	20.52	3014485
RING	18.61	2200000
EWZ	35.18	922633
GDX	22.97	2137930
VGK	56.38	513676

Let me zoom in on the Block Trade Indicator to show you the prints. There are three 500K share blocks in a row all at the same price of $49.47.

At the time, **PYPL** was trading way above that price, at $50.85.

Because the price of the print is much lower than the current trading price, we call these **late Dark Pool buy prints**. These are very sneaky trades that are very delayed. The big boys were buying and hiding their orders. We started to add onto our

PYPL long positions after spotting these late buy prints.

Let's go back to my live trading room so I can show you how we spotted these prints and called them out.

General Chat Transcript

Room Name: Java Pit
Date and Time: May 25 2017 04:34:17

The Cowboy entered his projected target for his **PYPL** swing.

09:19 **Cowboy**: PYPL project tgt 55.30ish

Cameron and I bought **PYPL** again. I bought the $52.50 strike June monthly calls.

Nitro noticed the **PYPL** prints that were very unusual.

09:38 **Cameron**: B PYPL again
09:39 **Stefanie Kammerman**: B PYPL lottos 52.50's June monthly

09:39 **Nitro**: PYPL prints 500k x2 @ 49.47

I confirmed that they were very late buy prints.

09:39 **Stefenie Kammerman**: Very late buy prints PYPL

Cathy looked back at her charts and posted that **PYPL** hadn't traded at this price since last Friday.

> **09:42 Cathy:** PYPL hasn't been at that price since last Friday, at least not in the regular session

PYPL had actually traded at that price on Monday, but mind you, this was on a Thursday. These prints were three days late.

The next day, on May 26, one of my traders announced that Motley Fool gave **PYPL** a thumbs up.

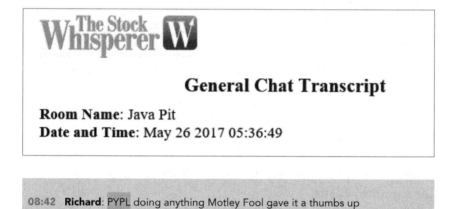

General Chat Transcript

Room Name: Java Pit
Date and Time: May 26 2017 05:36:49

> **08:42 Richard:** PYPL doing anything Motley Fool gave it a thumbs up

The Dark Pool prints always come first, before any news or any upgrades, or in this case, a thumbs up. Some of my traders took some profit, like Perry, who made 77 percent ROI.

> **10:55 Perry:** closed last 1/4 PYPL calls @ +77%

Other traders were holding onto their calls to higher targets, or like Bob, 'til death do us part.

> **13:37 Bob:** I'm holding PYPL until it hits 52.00 or I die. which ever occurs first

The stock went up even higher, and one trader had a huge win on this one. The Cowboy, who is 77 years young, made 600 percent ROI. By June 5, **PYPL** hit $53.85. Look at this next chart.

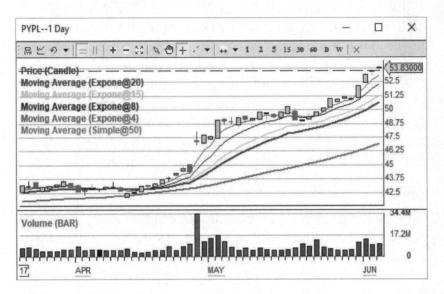

PYPL is a great example of how to trade a big print during a consolidation, but what happens if the price is only "consolidating" for a day or two? Let's take a look at candle patterns, and why I've found them to be so effective.

Candle Charts

While Japanese candlestick patterns are a great technical tool, it's what's inside the candle that really matters. My good friend and colleague Larry Berman told me a story that really brought this statement to life. He told me that on his first day of work on the floor of the New York Stock Exchange, he was asked by a market maker, **"What candle do you want me to make for you, Larry?"** Could it be that easy? Did these market makers try to fake us out by forming bullish candlesticks to try to get us to buy a stock? They could do this very easily by forming a candle pattern on low volume. Doing so on low volume would not cost too much money if they knew there was a huge sell order they needed to fill.

**RULE #1 - ONLY LOOK AT CANDLE PATTERNS THAT
ARE FORMED ON HIGH VOLUME.** A high-volume candle
costs too much money to fake us out. It's real volume. The most
important lesson I have learned over the years is that volume
is the holy grail. It does not matter what strategy you use; your
odds will always increase if there is high volume involved.
This is especially the case with Japanese Candlesticks. There is
always a good story behind each pattern. Each candle paints a
picture, and it's our job as traders to study them and trade off
them when the picture is finished.

For those of you who are brand new to candlesticks, I'm going
to quickly review the basics of a candle. However, I am going to
assume that most of you reading this book have some general
knowledge on candlesticks. You can Google images and find
tons of information on them. I also have a great workshop that I
have done called **"What's Inside the Candle."**

Let's quickly review the basics of a candle.

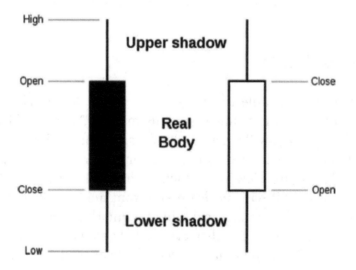

To create a candlestick chart, you must have a data set that contains where the stock opened, the high, the low, and the close of that time period. It doesn't matter what time frame you are using. A five-minute or 15-minute chart will give you a shorter-term candlestick pattern which is great to watch if you are doing very short-term trading. A daily or weekly candlestick pattern will give you a longer-term outlook. This is beneficial for longer-term swing trading.

It takes a lot more volume to form a candle on a daily or a weekly chart. Therefore, weekly candle patterns take precedence over daily charts, which take precedence over five-minute charts. Keep in mind that even if you are just day trading, your odds are going to be greater on your trade if the bigger weekly picture paints the same story.

Most charting software follows similar color conventions. If a candle closes below where it opened, the body of the candle will most likely be red or black. If a candle closes higher than where it opened, the body of the candle will most likely be white or green.

The shadows are the lows below and the highs above where the price action occurred that minute, day, or week depending on what timeframe you are using. These shadows are often referred to as wicks and tails. In general, tails on the bottom are buying, while wicks on the top are selling. This leads me to my next set of rules.

RULE #2 - NEVER BUY A STOCK AT THE END OF THE DAY WITH A BIG WICK AT THE TOP. That stock closed way off the high of the day. Sellers came in at the end of the day.

RULE #3 - BUY STOCKS ONLY IF THE STOCK CLOSES STRONG ON ABOVE-AVERAGE VOLUME. The same rule applies to the short side (Rule #5).

RULE #4 - NEVER SHORT A STOCK WITH A BIG WICK

ON THE BOTTOM. Buyers came in at the end of the day.

RULE #5 - SHORT STOCK ONLY IF THE STOCK CLOSES WEAK ON ABOVE AVERAGE VOLUME.

These were the first set of rules that I was taught on how to trade. To this day I still follow them; however, I've added a few extra Dark Pool twists to them.

Sometimes, candles can be indecisive or neutral. The story behind these candles is that there is a battle between the bulls and the bears. Nothing changed after the battle was over. The candle ends up closing exactly where it opened. We call this a doji candle. Look at this picture of quite a few different types of doji candles. They have different wicks and tails, but they have all managed to close exactly or pretty close to where it opened.

Doji's

| Doji | Long Legged Doji | Dragonfly Doji | Gravestone Doji |

Every one of these candle patterns represents balance between the buyers and sellers, but the shadows, or wicks, tell a slightly different story.

For a **Doji**, the wicks are relatively small and similar in size, and so all of its volume is in a small concentrated area. This type of candle formation on high volume tells the story of being "the calm before the storm." This small indecisive candle usually precedes a bigger move.

The **Long-legged Doji** has a lot more volatility on the day. This candle paints us a slightly different story. Even though it has had a bigger move that day, it still manages to close exactly where it opened. The difference is that the volume is not concentrated in a small space. Instead, the volume, as well as the price, is spread out. I find these candles are lot harder to trade. The only way we can get a huge advantage is if we have a huge print for which we can use as a level to trade.

The **Dragonfly Doji** is one of my favorite candles. This candle tells us a story of a possible trend change that might occur. **The most lucrative trades occur when the trend changes**. The story behind this candle is that the bears lost their swagger when the bulls moved in and bought the lower lows. Pegging the top or the bottom of a move can be very difficult, but if we have a possible reversal candle, that can change the storyline quickly. If price action closes above the high, it confirms a bullish trend reversal.

The **Gravestone Doji** is the opposite of the Dragonfly Doji since the opening and the closing price is at the low of the day. The story behind this candle is that the bulls have lost their swagger at the top of the uptrend. The bears have moved in and sold the stock down that day, creating what looks like a gravestone. This is considered to be a bearish reversal candle, but I prefer to have confirmation of a close below the low of the gravestone the next trading day. These candlestick patterns don't have that high of a success rate. According to many studies, they perform at only a 50 percent success rate. Therefore, following the Dark Pool prints inside the candle is our best way to trade. Let me show you how to do that. Here comes the fun part. We're going to take these doji indecision candles which do not have a high success rate by themselves, and we're going to add some Dark Pool prints to increase their success rate significantly.

Let's go back to the regular doji candle. Since dojis by themselves are indecision candles, it is best to wait and see what the next candle will bring.

High volume dojis are my favorite. That's a tug of war between massive amounts of bulls and bears where nobody wins because it closes unchanged. You need to wait until the next day or two and see if the candle can close above the high or below the low of that high volume doji candle. It's this easy: A close above is extremely bullish, and a close below is extremely bearish. Price action may go above or below during that day, creating what many traders call *"noise."* You need to wait and see where it closes. The close is the key.

Here is an example on Bank of America (**BAC**):

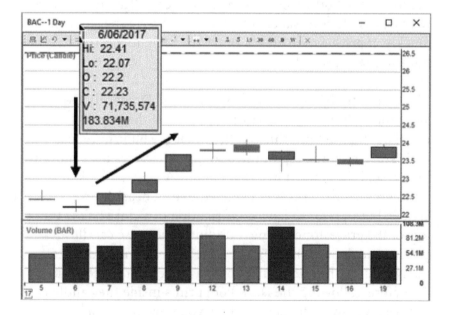

On June 6, 2017, **BAC** formed a high volume doji candle. It opened at $22.20 and closed at $22.23. Almost a perfect doji. There is a penny spread on **BAC** between the bid and the offer. After going up to a high of $22.41 and down to a low of $22.07, it managed to close very near to where it opened. Take a look at the volume that day. The volume was greater than the day before. A high-volume battle between the bulls and the bears occurred. It was most definitely the calm before the storm.

Guess what we spotted on that same day? There was a huge print on **BAC**. A 2.7 million block printed at **$22.36**, right near the end of the day. Only one hour of trading to go. Here is a picture of that trade:

Select or Input	BAC(W) Jun09 15.5 P (0)		
	BAC BAC(W) Jun09 15.5 P 06/06/2017		
⦿ Underlying trades			
Time ▲	**Symbol**	**Qty**	**Price**
09:30:03	BAC	653683	22.2000
15:09:17	BAC	2774256	22.3600

You can see there was another print for 653K at **$22.20**. In this type of situation, it's best to wait for the next day to jump in. We have two scenarios that can happen. We can close below the **$22.07** low of the day, which would also be below that massive print at **$22.36**. If that occurred, we would turn bearish and go short. The second scenario is that we close above the high of **$22.41**, which would also be above that massive print at **$22.36**. That would be bullish, and we would go long.

Here is a picture of the OHLC for the following day:

6/07/2017
Hi: 22.62
Lo: 22.265
O : 22.3
C : 22.6
V : 66,429,729
22.1603

You can see that on **June 7, BAC** opened up at **$22.30**, went down to make a low of **$22.26** but climbed back up to make a high of **$22.62** closing very strong at **$22.60**. This is what I call a **screaming long**. It closed above the high volume doji as well as the huge 2.7M print. I've found that combining candles and prints can greatly increase your success rate.

While most candlestick patterns have only a 50 to 60 percent success rates, there are a few patterns with a little bit higher success rate, around 70 percent. While 70 percent accuracy is much better than 50 percent, we still need to combine them with Dark Pool prints for a better trade. Trading by candle alone is not romantic enough for our profits.

One of my favorite candlestick patterns is the Abandoned Baby reversal pattern. The reason this is one of my favorites is because it is rare and predicts trend reversals with a 70 percent accuracy rate. Like the Dragonfly Doji, there are two types of Abandoned Babies: bullish and bearish.

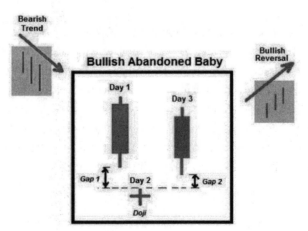

(Copyright © 2013-2016 All Rights Reserved. StockMarketStudent)

The bullish **Abandoned Baby reversal pattern** appears at the low of a downtrend, after a series of bearish candles printing lower lows and lower highs. The stock gaps lower on the next candle, but there are no more sellers which produces a small range doji candlestick. A bullish gap on the third candle completes this pattern. This creates a candle not overlapping in price levels from the candle before and the candle after.

There is also a bearish Abandoned Baby reversal pattern that looks like this:

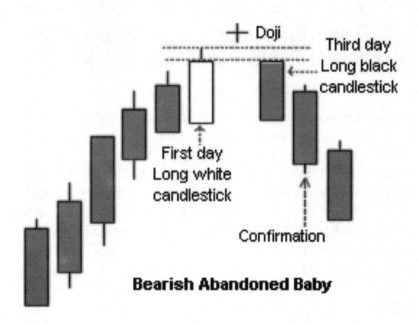

Bearish Abandoned Baby

Even though this is a rare pattern, I was able to find one on SSR Mining (**SSRI**). The symbol for this stock has since changed to **SSRM**. This company focuses on gold and silver mining.

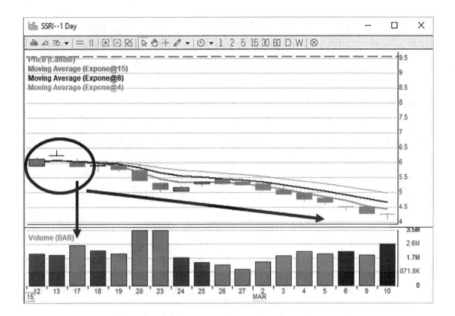

I have circled the bearish Abandoned Baby pattern on the chart. I have also drawn an arrow down to show you how volume increased on the last candle of this pattern. **SSRI** went down several dollars, confirming this bearish pattern. Increasing volume with these candlestick patterns is very important. There may be many smaller orders that add up to a big volume bar or there could be one huge print that happens within the candle. I couldn't find any large prints on **SSRI** on **February 17, 2015**, but I did find something very interesting. I found a huge Dark Pool sell print on the iShares Silver Trust ETF (**SLV**).

Select	SLV Feb20'15 1 P (0)		▼
or			
Input	SLV SLV Feb20'15 1 P 02/17/2015		

⦿ Underlying trades

Time ▲	Symbol	Qty	Price
09:30:00	SLV	224803	15.7400
09:30:00	SLV	224803	15.7400
10:08:14	SLV	65694	15.7000
10:08:53	SLV	73515	15.6700
10:17:16	SLV	63665	15.6600
10:23:11	SLV	82092	15.6600
11:44:26	SLV	1044944	15.7775

At 11:44am ET, over one million shares printed on **SLV** at $15.77. This is a highly unusual huge print which I call a gift. Even though we didn't get a print on **SSRI**, we got a great clue from a print on **SLV**, which is within the same sector as **SSRI**. The more highly unusual prints we get across multiple stocks within one sector, the higher our odds are when we enter that trade.

These Abandoned Babies are rare, so when you find one that has high volume, just know that you have found a diamond.

There is a more common candlestick pattern that has similar characteristics to the Abandoned Baby story. They are called **Evening Stars and Morning Stars**. The only difference between the Stars and the Babies is that the stars don't require a gap before and after the doji candle.

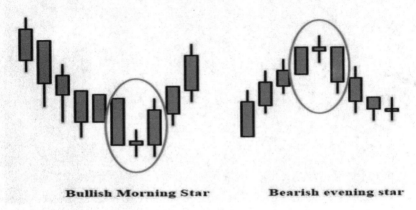

Bullish Morning Star   **Bearish evening star**

(Copyright © All Rights Reserved. Binary Option Sheriff University)

Let me give you an example of this. Kohl's Corporation (**KSS**) printed a bearish Evening Star pattern on the weekly chart. Since candlestick patterns are much stronger on the weekly chart, I found an Evening Star pattern that had a huge downward move afterwards.

Before we go into the technical chart of **KSS**, let's discuss the fundamentals for a minute. Retail has definitely had a tough time due to online shopping competition. Margins have gotten tighter and therefore many brick and mortar retailers have suffered quite a bit over the past few years. Okay, I think our minute is up.

Now let's look at the technical chart, so we can learn how to trade it.

I have circled the Evening Star pattern for you on this weekly chart. This pattern started on March 30, 2015, and ended on April 13, 2015. The three candles on the chart are those identified as MAR 30, APR 6, and APR 13.

This was a massive trend reversal for **KSS**. The stock went from
$80 down to a low of **$33.87**. We don't normally get anything
bigger than a 50K print on **KSS**, so seeing this trade for 239K
shares on March 31, 2015 at 1:30pm ET was a little unusual.

Select or Input	KSS Apr17'15 35 P (0) ▼
	KSS KSS Apr17'15 35 P 03/31/2015

⦿ Underlying trades

Time ▲	Symbol	Qty	Price
09:31:03	**KSS**	55697	76.6200
11:44:03	KSS	60276	78.7800
13:30:00	KSS	239390	79.0000

4/06/2015
Hi: 79.6
Lo: 77.25
O : 78.72
C : 78.4
V : 11,658,013
73.2547
AVG:74.543
AVG:77.095
AVG:60.308
AVG:54.072
AVG:66.546

Note that **KSS** closed under that print level
of $79 that week. That is always a bearish
sign. **KSS** closed at **$78.40** for the week. We
have a very bearish candlestick pattern with
an unusually large print on a weekly chart.
It doesn't get any better than this. This is
a **screaming short**. The best place to short
a stock is below the print. If this was a day
trade, we would short just below the print
around $78.99 and the best place to put our
stop is just above the print, which in this
trade would be at $79.03. If this was a swing
trade, we would want to make sure that it closed below the
print before going short. No matter what kind of trade you are
doing, you always want to make sure that you are on the right
side of the print!

Now I would like to introduce you to the **Hanging Man** pattern.

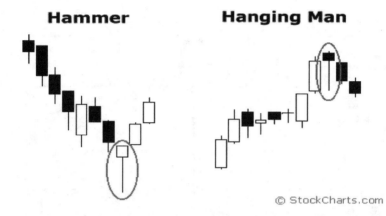

The Hanging Man pattern is a hammer candle that is found at the top of an uptrend. The story behind the Hanging Man is that the price opens near the high, then drops down much lower before clawing its way back up again. This pattern performs best in a bear market for a bearish reversal. <u>For confirmation, I like to see the price close below the entire candle.</u>

Look at this weekly chart of Halliburton (**HAL**):

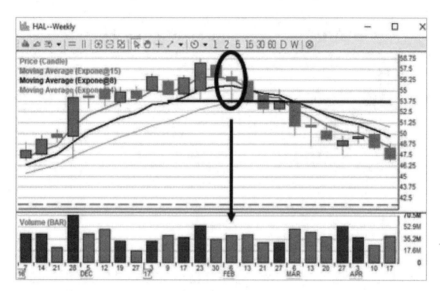

I've circled the Hanging Man at the top of the hill. I've also drawn a line at the low of that Hanging Man candle. Once **HAL** closed below that black line ($53.50), it rolled down the hill. Guess what we had at the top of the hill? Yes. Prints. We had some Dark Pool sell prints. These are some of the prints from **January 27, 2017**:

Individual option trades			
Select	HAL(W) Jan27 44 P (0)		▼
or Input	HAL HAL(W) Jan27 44 P 01/27/2017		
Underlying trades			

Time ▲	Symbol	Qty	Price
12:33:36	HAL	240000	58.0500
12:57:43	HAL	375000	58.0000

Two large blocks came in on January 27, totaling 615K at approximately $58.00. **HAL** never closed above that price after the Hanging Man formed. **HAL** came all the way down to $38. That was a huge $20 move to the downside.

There are prints at the top when the Dark Pool is selling, and there are prints at the bottom when the Dark Pool is buying.

On September 5, 2017, we spotted the largest prints that we've ever seen on **HAL**. Four million printed at $39.65. Here is what I wrote in my trading room:

13:40 **Stefanie Kammerman**: MASSIVE print $HAL 4 mil $39.65 Bullish above 40 Bearish below 39.50

I loved this trade so much I put it in my *"**Whisper of the Day**"* video the next day, on September 6, 2017.

#whisperoftheday9-6-17

The Stock Whisperer @ The Java Pit •

498 views • 2 months ago

The Stock Whisperer's Morning Whisper is: $SPY $XLE $XLP $HAL $AMD #morningwhisper

You can watch this video online at https://www.youtube.com/user/thestockwhisperer

We also spotted huge prints on Energy Sector SPDR ETF
(**XLE**). **HAL** is one of its top 10 holdings. Let me show you
those prints.

Individual option trades			
Select	HAL(W) Sep08 30 P (0)		
or Input	HAL HAL(W) Sep08 30 P 09/05/2017		
Underlying trades			

Time ▲	Symbol	Qty	Price
13:37:02	HAL	4080000	39.6500

Select	XLE(W) Sep08 56 P (0)		
or Input	XLE XLE(W) Sep08 56 P 09/05/2017		
Underlying trades			

Time ▲	Symbol	Qty	Price
09:49:29	XLE	151551	64.0000
11:06:51	XLE	229900	64.1190
15:22:21	XLE	2090000	63.9100

These prints were enormous. Here is what I wrote in my trading
room after we spotted the prints on **XLE**.

15:25 **Stefanie Kammerman**: Massive prints on $XLE 2 mil $63.91 Bullish above 64
Bearish below 63.75.

My trading room traded oil all month long on the long side. Here is a low risk trade I posted up in my live trading room on **HAL**.

13:42 **Stefanie Kammerman**: B lotto HAL calls 41.50's sept 15th exp
13:42 **Stefanie Kammerman**: I will add above 40

I went out of the money buying "lottery ticket" $41.50 strike calls, expiring the next week. These were cheap. The only reason you would buy these "lotto" options, as we call them in the trading room, is if you expected a big move to happen quickly. The only way that happens is when the Dark Pool is buying.

By pointing out unusual trades all day long and showing my traders the types of trades they can put on real time, my traders learn very quickly how to trade around the Dark Pool. It doesn't matter if you trade stock or options. The most important thing is learning what level to enter and exit.

This chart of **HAL** shows explosive movement to the upside after those prints:

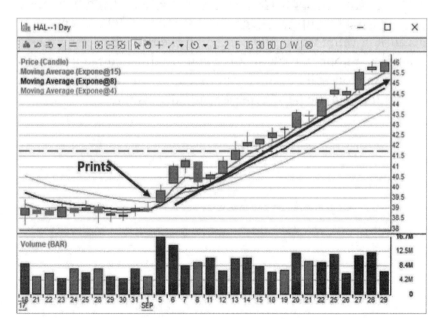

XLE also had a power move to the upside, shown on this chart:

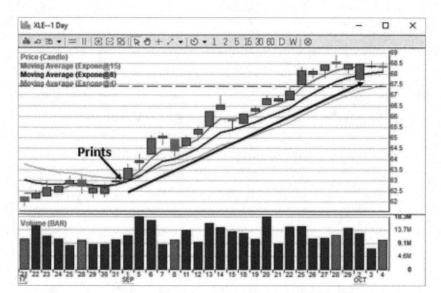

I could probably write a whole book on combining candlestick patterns with prints, but I have only dedicated one chapter of this book to it. It doesn't matter what technical tool you are using. <u>When you apply Dark Pool volume to it, it can increase your success rate up to 90 percent</u>. I stopped at 90 percent, because nothing works 100 percent of the time. By seeing these examples, I hope that by the time you are finished reading this book, that you will be convinced that applying these prints to your trades will help to increase your success rate.

I do have one last favorite candle pattern to show you:
The Bull Doji Sandwich.

WARNING: this pattern may make you hungry to trade!

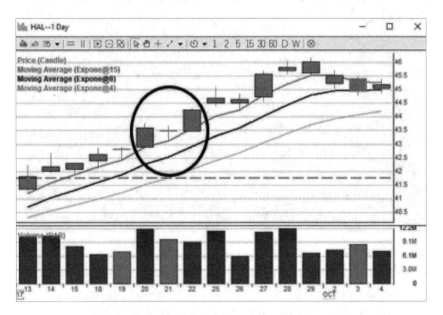

This is a very bullish three-candle pattern. The first candle
is a green bullish candle followed by a doji indecision candle
followed by a green bullish candle. This three-candle pattern
usually has more continuation to the upside.

Guess what we spotted? I think you guessed it right. Prints! We spotted a lot of prints on the doji candle on September 21, 2017.

Select or Input	HAL(W) Sep22 32 P (0)		
	HAL HAL(W) Sep22 32 P 09/21/2017		

Underlying trades

Time ▲	Symbol	Qty	Price
10:11:53	HAL	274000	43.3500
11:33:50	HAL	500000	43.4450
11:47:40	HAL	240000	43.5250
12:32:40	HAL	182000	43.4650
12:57:51	HAL	187200	43.4950

All day long we got some nice prints on **HAL** between $43.35 and $43.52. This doji was an indecision candle with some nice prints. Closing above these prints the next day was our confirmation. **Remember, it's what's inside the candle that matters**.

> *Stefanie Kammerman is a master tape reader and technical analyst. She goes out of her way to assist traders in learning her trading style and method. Stefanie can help you spot areas of accumulation that are not easily detectable by conventional trading tactics. Using her methods, you will learn how to risk a small amount in order to make substantial profits. I took a trade on GE in June 2017 that yielded 744 percent return on investment!*
>
> *Eli Carlin, Member of Stefanie Kammerman's Java Pit Trading Room*

Chapter 5

PRINTS, PIVOTS AND PATTERNS

Prints, pivots and patterns are the three amigos. The Trifecta. The Jackpot! When they're working together, you have the holy grail of trading. Trading is about PAY-tience. It's about waiting for the right set-ups. It's about waiting for the trade to come to you. These set-ups don't happen every day, but when they do, it's magical.

In this chapter, I'm going to show you examples of how pivot points, price patterns and my own T-Spot pattern work in conjunction with big prints to help you significantly increase your odds of success.

Pivot Points

The dictionary defines a pivot as the central point, pin, or shaft on which a mechanism turns or oscillates.

Years ago, we use to have real traders on the exchange floor instead of high frequency computers. These floor traders used pivots to trade off of for many years. Floor traders' pivots are support/resistance levels. They define an equilibrium point (considered a neutral market) called the pivot point or central pivot. The market is considered bullish when it's above the central pivot. It's considered bearish when it's below.

At the beginning of the trading day, floor traders would look at the previous day's high, low, and close to calculate a pivot point for the current trading day. With this pivot point as the base, further calculations were used to set Support 1, Support 2, Support 3, Resistance 1, Resistance 2 and Resistance 3. These levels would be used by these traders throughout the trading day.

Nowadays, the computers are doing all the trading and guess what? They are programmed to trade off these pivots. It's a self-fulfilling prophecy. While there are a few different pivot calculations, my personal favorites are Person's and Camarilla Pivots.

Here are some simple formulas to show how pivots are calculated:

Pivot Point	(P)	=	(High + Low + Close)/3
Support 1	(S1)	=	(P x 2) - High
Support 2	(S2)	=	P - (High - Low)
Resistance 1	(R1)	=	(P x 2) - Low
Resistance 2	(R2)	=	P + (High - Low)

Let me show you how we can combine the prints and the pivots to enter and exit trades. On October 11, 2017, we spotted an enormous print on Target (**TGT**). At 10:08am, 1.8 million shares printed at $58.75.

Here is the actual print on **TGT** in my LIVEVOL® Pro software:

Time ▲	Symbol	Qty	Price	Exchange
10:08:36	TGT	1850000	58.7500	NQNX

Input: TGT TGT(W) Oct13 48 P 10/11/2017 — Go — Underlying trades

This was highly unusual, so I had to Whisper about it.

The Weekly Whisper Video from the Dark Pool: CZR, TGT
10/12/2017 3:54 pm EST
Stefanie Kammerman, the Stock Whisperer, to tell you the Whisper of the Week: Caesars Palace and Target in my weekly Thursday video under five minutes and transcript. Get Trading Insights, MoneySho...

Tickers: CZR | TGT | MNST | SLV

This video is up on our website if you would like to listen to it.

I posted the trade up in my trading room as well, in the announcement tab.

10:14 Stefanie Kammerman: Unusual Huge print $TGT 1.8 mil $58.75 Bullish above 59 Bearish below 58.50

Here is the daily chart of **TGT** from October 11. I noted in the Whisper and the announcement that **TGT** was bullish above $59. You can see it closed above $59.

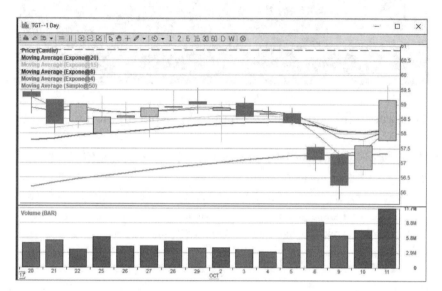

Here is the Open, High, Low, Close (OHLC) from that day:

10/11/2017
Hi: 59.67
Lo: 57.73
O: 57.79
C: 59.15
V: 11,676,598
58.7015
AVG:58.140
AVG:58.194
AVG:58.106
AVG:58.112
AVG:57.340

You can see it closed at $59.15, above the $58.75 print, as well as above the $59 level. This is what we call a screaming BUY.

Note that the volume was extremely high that day as well, topping out above 11 million shares. The 50-day average daily volume for **TGT** is about 6.8 million, so this represented over 150 percent average daily volume.

Before I show you the pivots from the next day on **TGT**, I need to share with you a common pattern that happens with these large prints. It's called a retest. So many times, after a big print happens, the stock will rally upwards. The stock then comes back down to "test" the print. Sometimes it may do a few retests before going up and making the real big move. They are testing to see if there is still demand at that lower price before really moving it up. Sometimes, they are bringing it back down to buy more at this level because they didn't get all the shares they wanted at that price. This retest is exactly what happened with **TGT** the next day. This is a great opportunity for traders who couldn't get into the trade before to enter on the retest.

Look at this 5-minute chart of **TGT** and note how it came down to that big print level of $58.75:

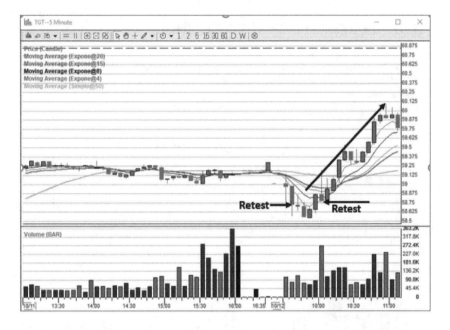

Sometimes, these stocks will test the level and fail, moving lower. In those cases, we would turn bearish. In the case of **TGT**, even though it went slightly lower than the print, **TGT** never went below our bearish level of $58.50. We need to give these stocks a little bit of room, so we use these specific levels.

You can see after the retest that **TGT** rallied up to $60. Ten dollar increment levels are strong, so $60 is a huge resistance level. Computers are programmed to sell at the $10, $5, and $1 increment levels. The first time around, we expect sellers. The second time a resistance level is reached, there will be fewer sellers. The third time, there will typically be even fewer sellers. The odds that it will break higher increases with each test. Some stocks, if they are really strong, may clear resistance on the second test. Others may require multiple tests. Weak stocks may not be able to break resistance at all.

TGT was pretty strong. The next day, on Friday, October 13, **TGT** rallied above $60, and climbed as high as $61.56.

Look at the 5-minute chart from that day:

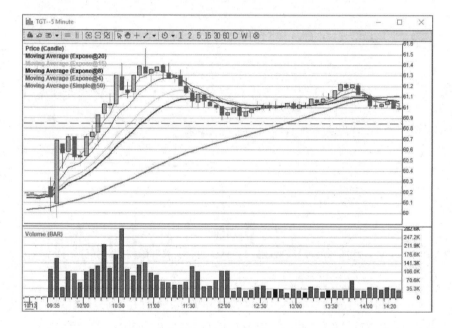

Why did it stop right there at \$61.56? This is where the pivots come in. Look at this next chart on the pivots that day for **TGT**:

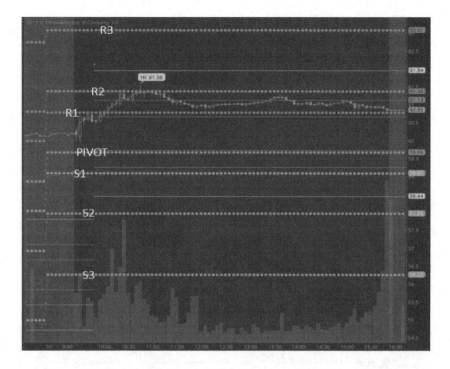

The stock stopped right at that Resistance 2 (R2) dotted line like a brick wall. This happens all day long. Stock will ping pong back and forth on the pivots. I love to trade off the pivots knowing that this is where computers are loaded to buy and sell. Keep in mind, this is just one example. I see examples of this all the time. I could write ten books on them.

Price Patterns

Let's go more in depth with patterns. The brain not only receives information but interprets and patterns it. When it comes to technical analysis, patterns are the distinctive formations created by the movements of security prices on a chart. A pattern can be identified by a line connecting common price points (such as closing prices, highs, or lows) over a period. On a candle chart, candle patterns can form in as little as one period.

The basic technical analysis patterns that most of you have heard of include head and shoulders, inverse head and shoulders, bull and bear flags, falling and rising wedges, rounded bottoms, triple top and triple bottom reversals, ascending and descending triangles, cup and handle. You may be familiar with many more. This book isn't about simple technical analysis patterns. You can search Google for that and find pictures for all those patterns. I would like to teach you the pattern of how to apply Dark Pool prints along with volume to your channel trend lines to achieve the highest success rates.

Let's go over trend lines first. Finding support and resistance is an essential part of trading. Most traders are taught to draw horizontal support and resistance lines. That's okay when a stock is consolidating like this next chart of Lululemon (**LULU**):

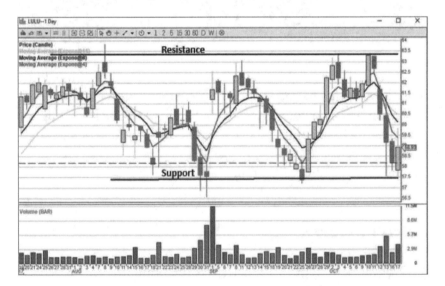

When stocks are going sideways, there is no trend. When there is no trend, drawing two major lines is all you need. Draw support and draw resistance. When stocks are trending, as in this next chart of PayPal (**PYPL**), we need to draw channel trend lines. The two parallel diagonal lines are mapping out the pattern of where the stock is going if it moves higher. The lower line shows support, and the higher one shows resistance. I have also drawn arrows pointing down to volume to show you how each time **PYPL** hit one of these trend lines, volume increased from the previous day. This is a very popular pattern because computers are programmed to buy and sell when a stock hits these channel lines.

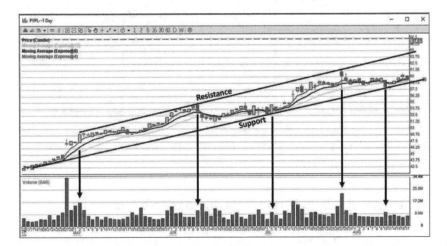

Just as we have upward trend lines, we also have downward trend lines. Look at this next chart of General Electric (**GE**):

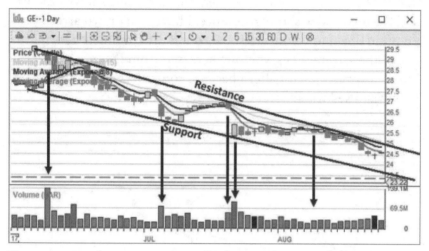

You can see that every time **GE** hit support and resistance, the volume increased.

Many times, when a stock hits one of these channel lines, we see nice prints to go along with that. Let me show you an example on Starbucks (**SBUX**). On August 21, 2017, we spotted a very large print in the middle of the day on **SBUX**. A block print of 527K shares came in at $53.38. This was highly unusual.

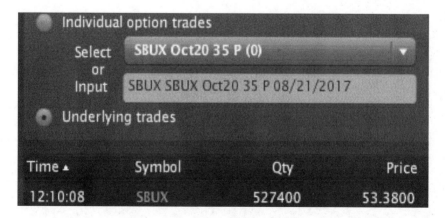

Now look at the chart of **SBUX**. You'll see that **SBUX** had just bounced off the bottom trend line when this big print happened.

Guess what happened the next time it came down to that bottom trend line on September 8? That same computer was still buying. There were two more huge prints, 1.28M and 400K, both at $53.35. This is a popular pattern. Look at these prints:

Select or Input	SBUX Oct20 35 P (0) ▼
	SBUX SBUX Oct20 35 P 09/08/2017

⬤ Underlying trades

Time ▲	Symbol	Qty	Price
11:40:57	SBUX	400000	53.3500
11:40:57	SBUX	1275980	53.3500

I liked this so much I put it into my popular Whisper of the Day video on September 11.

> **#whisperoftheday9-11-17**
> The Stock Whisperer @ The Java Pit • 511 views • 1 month ago
>
> The Stock Whisperer's Morning Whisper is: $T $SBUX $SPY #morningwhisper #hotstockoftheday #todayswhisper #whisperoftheday. For more please visit me at

It happened again. The next time **SBUX** came down to the bottom trend line, the computers were still buying. This time on September 29, they bought 300K at $53.57.

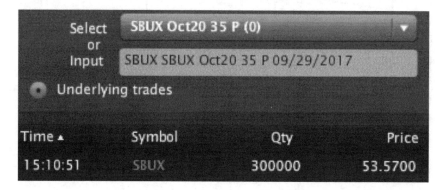

Select or Input	SBUX Oct20 35 P (0)		
	SBUX SBUX Oct20 35 P 09/29/2017		
⦿ Underlying trades			
Time ▲	Symbol	Qty	Price
15:10:51	SBUX	300000	53.5700

I find following prints and patterns give me the highest probability trades. When I see prints coming at these channel lines, this is one of my favorite patterns to trade. For intraday trading, we want to also use our pivots along with levels to enter and exit at the most optimal times.

T-Spot Pattern

Years ago, I did a workshop called "How to Find the T-Spot." Many traders emailed me to tell me that the only way they could take this class was if their wives sat next to them. Apparently, they were suspicious that I was teaching something that wasn't related to trading.

The T-spot is what I refer to as the trend change spot. What do you think they were thinking? The T-spot is the exact spot on your chart where the trend changes from uptrend to downtrend or downtrend to uptrend. This spot is the money spot. This is where the stock will usually get a huge reversal. Almost every book on how to trade will tell you to follow the trend. The trend is your friend. The trend is your friend except at the end. Follow the trend until the trend changes. This is all great advice, but how do we know when the trend has changed?

I always assumed that everybody was a master at drawing trend lines on charts. I found out early on that most traders needed a little extra help. The best way to draw a trend line would be to start at the very peak of the chart and draw a line downward touching as many peaks as you can. The more candles you touch, the stronger that trend line.

Here is a great example on the weekly chart of Caterpillar (**CAT**). You can see we touched three peaks with this downward trend line.

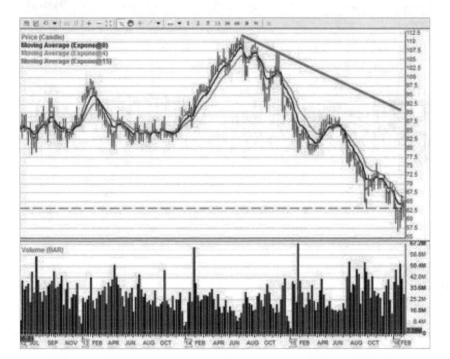

Next, we are going to draw another trendline, but this time we are going to touch as many valleys as we can. Where these two lines intersect will be the T-spot. X marks the spot. On this chart of **CAT**, that price is marked at $107.50. Once **CAT** dropped below $107.50, the trend changed from uptrend to downtrend. The only way to change this trend would have been to break above $107.50, which **CAT** was unable to do. Instead, the price dropped much lower.

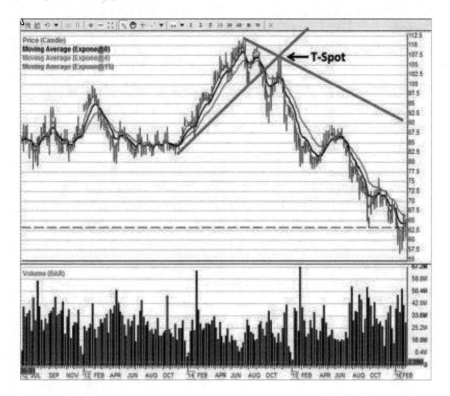

There's more than one T-spot on this chart. Let me show you. We will draw another downward trend line touching the recent peaks along with another upward trend line. Where these two lines intersect is another T-spot at $87.50. On this next chart, **CAT** would need to break above $87.50 to change the trend from downward to upward trend. You can see it was unable to do that, and it continued rolling down the hill to around $57.50.

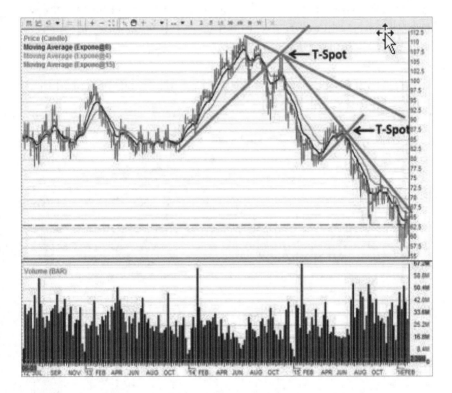

It just so happened that I was doing a live stage presentation in New York February 23, 2016, at the TradersEXPO, when **CAT** was at these prices. I was teaching the audience how to find the T-spot. My presentation was called "To Swing or Not To Swing." I know what you're thinking. I didn't think this was a dirty presentation when I wrote it, but I will tell you it drew a lot of attention. All the seats were taken; standing room only.

I expressed to the audience that the only way we should buy
CAT is if it can break above that last downward trend line
we just drew. This stock would need to break above $67.50 to
change this very long downward trend. I even went as far as to
map out the trades for them if it happened. I believe we should
always be prepared as a trader.

There were two trade setups. The first trade was from $67.50
to $80.00. I drew a straight line across the chart at $80 to show
that this was a heavy resistance line. What was once support
was now acting as resistance.

If **CAT** could break above $80, the next trade set up would be
from $80 to $87.50.

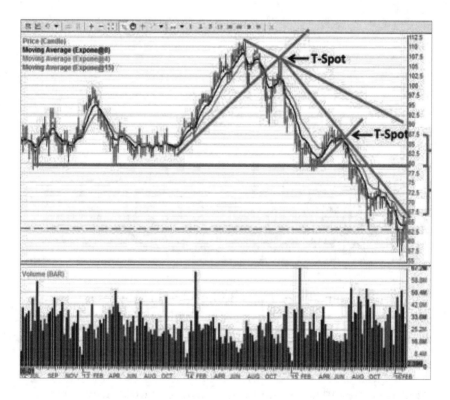

Coincidentally, **CAT** broke the T-spot the week after I did this presentation. Talk about great timing. We called this trade out in our trading room as soon as **CAT** broke above $67.50. On February 29, 2016, **CAT** closed above $67.50.

Here is the chat from the next day, March 1, at 11:14am ET, where I called out the trade. B **CAT** Call, above $67.50, T-spot, 1st target is $72.50. I posted that as **CAT** was above the $67.50 T-spot, that it was a good time to buy call options on **CAT**.

3-1 Chat.pdf		31 / 111	Ċ	⊃	⊟
[11:02] Cowboy:	Jack time				
[11:02] John Y:	Ricki don't lose that number as an into				
[11:02] Wesley F:	green drink time here in California				
[11:03] Celeste:	happy hour in Canada				
[11:03] Cowboy:	She did great				
[11:03] Terry T:	I worship at the church of Ricki because all I trade is options. :-) Preach it girl! lol				
[11:04] John Y:	thanks				
[11:05] Colton F:	so someone else actually does sell premium?!				
[11:06] Celeste:	bless you Ricki				
[11:06] Colton F:	for sure				
[11:07] Colton F:	I enjoy doing it, trying to find a good, consistent strategy with it				
[11:07] Celeste:	court sided with apple				
[11:08] Ron F:	good point				
[11:08] Denis B:	KIN 9.00 - 841k				
[11:10] BeachBoy:	ROST tonite				
[11:10] Stefanie K:	CAT above t-spot				
[11:10] Celeste:	bullish				
[11:11] Terry T:	YHOO new HOD				
[11:11] Baker V:	Can you talk about how you approach an earnings trade?				
[11:13] Liquid Assets:	strangles/straddle work for earnings				
[11:13] Celeste:	is your horse ok now?				
[11:14] Stefanie K:	B CAT call, above 67.50 T-spot, 1st tgt is 72.50 ←				

Let me enlarge that post so you can see it better.

(11:14) Stefanie K: B CAT call, above 67.50 T-spot, 1st tgt is 72.50 ⬅

It took only three days to hit our hit our first target of $72.50. On April 19, **CAT** hit our T-spot $80 target. Look at the chart and note that the 4 EMA crossed over the 8 EMA on the weekly chart. **CAT** rode the 4 EMA up for most of the time. A popular pattern that occurs is that after riding the 4 train for a while, it will pull back to the 8 EMA before riding the 4 train once again. That is exactly what happened to **CAT**: high speed momentum at its best.

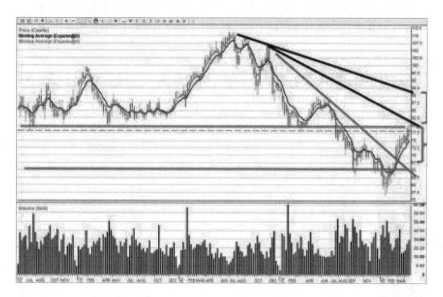

After hitting resistance at $80, **CAT** pulled back, only to rally back up again and hit our second target of $87.50. It went much higher than $87.50. This was a great trade off the T-spot!

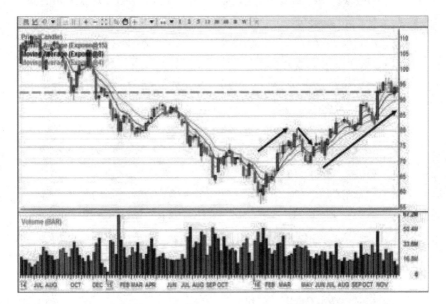

Sometimes you must wait a few minutes for a great trade set up to happen and sometimes you must wait a year. In this case, we waited a year. Patience and discipline are two key requirements to achieve success at trading.

I used to have my money handled by a financial advisor. It drove me crazy how much I was paying in commissions and my portfolio wasn't increasing. A very successful friend of mine told me to move my money into a self-directed account and he would help me with my investments (for free!). I started following stocks on StockTwits and was so fascinated by it all. I wanted to learn more. Over the next 4 years, I took 4 boot camps with 4 different people. All different styles but none of them made me a successful trader. I realized that I didn't want to be a "follower"... I wanted to really understand the trades. I lost a lot of money during those 4 years but I learned a lot. As they say... you learn from your mistakes. I found Stefanie on StockTwits. I followed along with her "Whisper of the Day" and saw how consistent she was. I joined her chat room and quickly realized that I needed to take her boot camp. I took her boot camp 1 year ago. What I learned from her was life changing. Following the prints works.

Stefanie has taught me how to follow the prints. I can now trade on my own and I don't have to "follow" anyone. I wish I would have met Stefanie 4 years ago when I started trading. It would have saved me a lot of money. She is a great teacher... as well as a very caring person. Even though she is trading herself all day long, she will always take the time to answer questions and to explain things. She comes on the microphone twice a day and I write down everything she says. Every day, she gives someone the title of "Trader of the Day". I have received this award a couple of times now and it truly is an honour to be recognized by her!! I will never leave her trading room since I learn from her every single day. She is truly AMAZING!!!

Jan L.

Chapter 6

10 RULES FOR TRADING THE DARK POOLS

There is a specific set of 10 rules that I follow when searching for a Whisper. For those of you who don't like to follow rules, you're in luck because my rule #10 gives you permission to break all of the earlier nine rules. We all need a rule like that. I'm going to share with you all 10 of my rules. I challenge you to follow them. I hope you do follow them.

Rule #1 - Monitor Pre-Market Volume

Does your trading platform have premarket volume? Are you able to see what is trading before the regular market hours? The opening bell sounds at 9:30am Eastern Time, but some stocks will start trading as early as 4:00am. Most people are not aware that the market trades before the opening bell. Not all stocks trade pre-market, but often times, the big guys are already giving us clues as to what stocks are going to be hot that day by trading them before the market opens. If you do not have software that shows you premarket volume, you are missing these clues. So how much volume do we need to see? I look for at least 100K shares traded before the market is even opened. This tells me that there is real heavy interest in that stock. This creates momentum. My biggest secret is premarket momentum. These voluminous stocks are going to shoot up like a rocket… or crash down as soon as the market opens. Most importantly, the premarket volume shows us what levels the big boys are loaded to buy and sell. This is how I find my levels: bullish above, bearish below, no thinking.

Here is a great example of premarket volume on Bank of America (**BAC**) September 13, 2017:

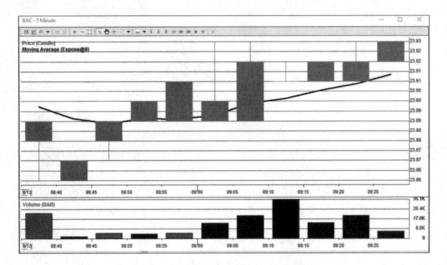

This is the 5-minute chart from 8:30am to 9:30am, the last hour before the market officially opened. You can see from the volume bars at the bottom of the chart that **BAC** traded well over 100K before the open. The highest spike of volume occurred at around 9:10am. If **BAC** stays above that buying volume at $23.92, we will be bullish. I like to take it one step further and go to the next level up which is $24. In my Whisper that day, I used the $24 level as you will see shortly.

In my early days as an overnight swing trader, I learned the best way to exit my positions using volume as my #1 indicator. When stocks would gap up on very little volume Pre-Market, we would exit Pre-Market. We called this a "pop and drop." This is how the big guys try to fake out the little guys. They try to prop up the stock price with nothing but air. Stocks need real volume to keep them flying higher.

Here is a picture of a "pop and drop" on JetBlue Airways Corporation (**JBLU**):

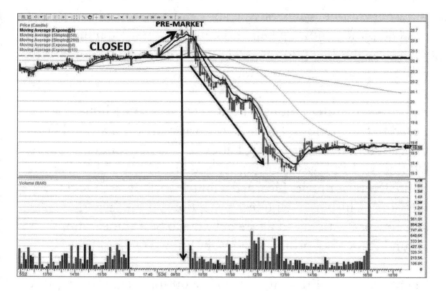

During the premarket hours, **JBLU** was trading 30 cents higher than the previous day's close. As you can see, there was not much volume to keep it up there. It dropped like a rock as soon as the market opened. Make sure you pay attention to how much volume your stock is trading premarket. Let's move on to our second rule.

Rule #2 - Only Day Trade the Stock When the Price is Under $40

The great thing about trading Dark Pool prints is that you don't have to just trade the stock. If I find a great opportunity on a stock that is priced under $40, I'll trade the stock. However, if the price is over $40, I like to trade options on the stock because it reduces my risk and enables me to control the stock without actually owning it.

While some option commentators out there are waiting for "unusual volume" when buying and selling options. Dark Pool prints typically show up before the move. You'll often find that you've caught the option market off-guard and paid a lower price than you would have if you waited.

Before we dig into options, I need to confess something to you. I used to hate options. I could never wrap my head around how to profit off them. Every time I attended classes about options, I felt like my head was spinning around like Linda Blair's character in the Exorcist movie. I learned a lot by working with Ricki, the "Options Whisperer," who teaches options in my Java Pit. I was able to work with her to figure out how to best trade options around Dark Pool prints. As a result, I now LOVE options!

There are many different ways to use options, but the simplest strategy is to buy calls or puts. The reason this works, is that this strategy has you buy when the options are cheap. In order to make money with directional options trades you need to get four things right:

1. Pick the right stock
2. Choose the right direction
3. Pick the best strike
4. Figure out how fast it will move

Many options are not liquid so it's important to pick the right stock. With illiquid stocks, their options have large bid/ask spreads because nobody is trading them. There is nothing worse than being in a trade all by yourself.

Trading Dark Pool prints makes it relatively easy to choose the right direction, that's why I dedicated a whole chapter to it. Bullish above, bearish below. No thinking!

Once you have the right stock and established a direction for the price, the next step is to pick the best strike. As an options trader, you need to decide whether to go in-the-money (**ITM**) or out-of-the-money (**OTM**). When you go out of the money, you're going to pay less for the option, because you're not paying for intrinsic value. I personally like to pay less, but these trades won't make any money unless the stock moves close to the **OTM** strike. The key to trading these **OTM** options is knowing that our stock is going to have a big move.

Lastly, you must figure out how fast it will move. Is it going to take a few hours, a few days, a few weeks or longer? Timing matters because you need to choose the options series, or rather the options expiration, that best fits your expectations.

Rule #3 - Only Day Trade Stocks That Have a Penny Spread

There are plenty of stocks from which to choose that are under $40 that make nice intraday moves and that have only a penny spread between the bid and the offer. Stocks that have more than a penny spread are dangerous. The risk is too high. A two-cent spread can turn into a five- or eight-cent spread in a few seconds.

This next picture is a Level 2 quote on Adamas
Pharmaceutical (**ADMS**):

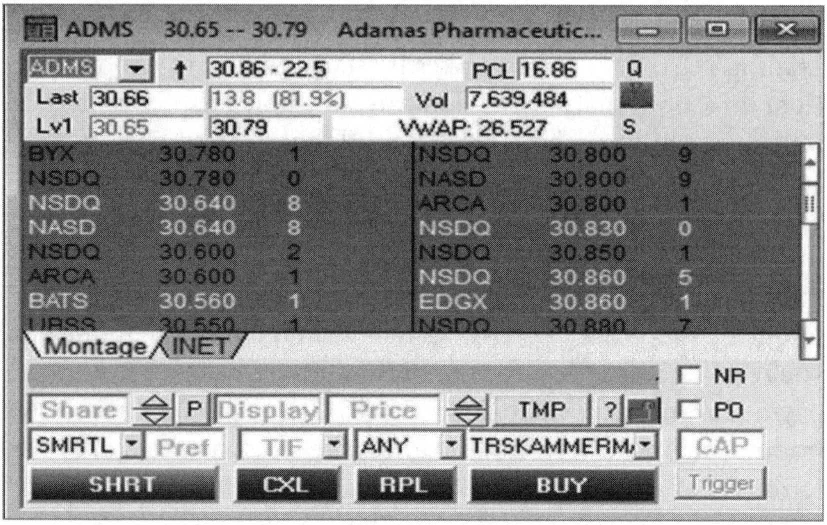

The bid is $30.78 and the offer is $30.80. That's a two-cent
spread. What's so dangerous about that? It doesn't look that
dangerous, but look what happened in the next few seconds.

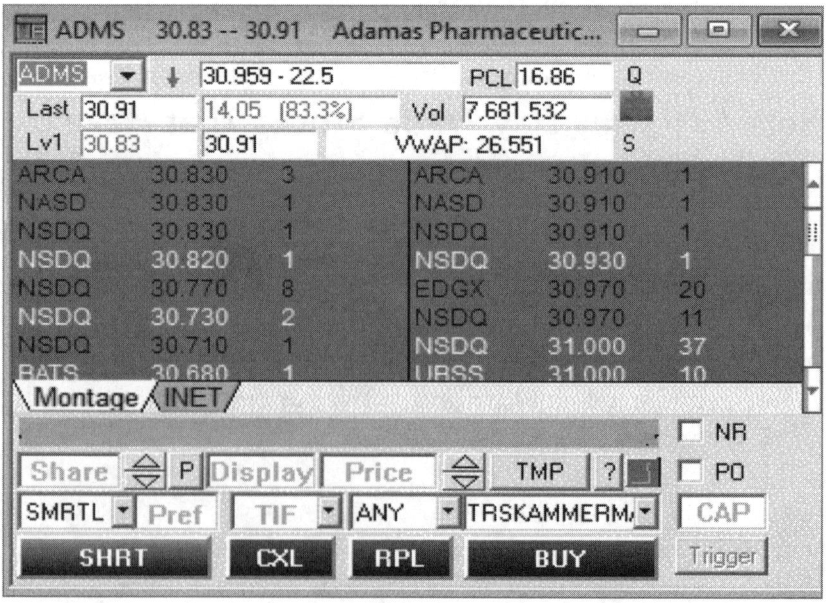

The spread widened quickly. While the bid went up five cents to $30.83, the offer went up 11 cents to $30.91. The two-cent spread is now an eight-cent spread. While the entry looked benign, it's much more difficult to exit profitably when the bid/ask spread is eight cents.

I have another rule that is not on my checklist. All my traders are fully aware of this rule. I do not do drugs. This example of **ADMS** shows one of the reasons I don't trade drug stocks. In addition to widening spreads, these drug stocks, as a sector, have gained notoriety for two other reasons.

Not a day goes by that we do not wake up and see a biotech stock crushed down 10 percent or more. There have been some that have lost nearly 80 percent in value overnight. Over the years I have known great traders who have gotten completely wiped out by one stock. That stock was always a biotech stock. This is the highest risk sector to trade. Secondly, these stocks can also get halted at any time due to bad news. I will not trade biotech/pharmaceutical stocks.

If you truly want to be a successful trader, your main concern should be about controlling your risk. Risk management should always come ahead of consideration for how much money you can make off a trade. Our next rule is all about patience.

Rule #4 - Time Your Entry

Do not trade the first 10- to 15-minute period of the trading day. I am sure many of you may have experienced this at some point in your trading career. The opening bell rings. The market starts to really move. You feel like you are missing the party. You chase it, entering right at the top of the move. It's almost as if somebody is watching you buy it because as soon as you buy it, it stops moving higher. A second later, it drops like a rock. You then panic, selling it right at the low of the move only to watch it move up again. If this sounds familiar to you, you are not alone. If you just wait 10 to 15 minutes after the open, you're more likely to avoid this volatility and let a nice easy trade come to you.

The best time to enter a day trade is from 9:45-11am. That hour-and-fifteen minute period has the best momentum bounce. After 11am, momentum dries up. Picture a ball rolling off a table. That first bounce is going to be nice and big. That first bounce is our best trades from 9:45-11am. The second bounce isn't going to be as big as the first bounce. That bounce is from 11am-12pm. The third bounce is going to be even smaller. I typically recommend that you don't enter a new trade after 11am. However, after 2pm momentum starts to pick up again. The last 25 minutes can also be a great time to enter a new day trade or an overnight momentum swing trade. I will go into further details on swing trading in a later chapter.

I usually don't like to day trade at the end of the day unless it is earnings season. During earnings season, we will find some amazing day trades at the end of the day. Stocks that are going to report after the close will sometimes move on pre-earnings momentum. They will have one last nice move up or down before they close. You must be very careful not to hold a stock into earnings. That is gambling. Even if you knew what the earnings were going to be, you can never be sure of how the stock will react. We have seen stocks come out with great earnings only to get crushed. We've seen stocks come out with horrible earnings that will rally. The best trades we have taken during earnings season are when these stocks change from positive to negative, or negative to positive. Many times, the stock already has priced in the expected earnings report and is now trading on future expectations. The day after earnings is often times our favorite time to day trade these stocks. The volatility is amazing.

There are days where we can trade all day long because of the wonderful volatility. Keep in mind, however, these are rare days. Don't overtrade on days that aren't good. Lucky for us, earnings season comes four times a year. Early to mid-January, April, July, and October. In between the earnings season is when we love to swing trade.

Swinging stocks overnight during earnings season can be very risky. Your stock, or another stock in the same sector, may have an earnings warning. Even if it's not your stock announcing a pre-earnings warning, your stock will go down in sympathy with that stock most of the time. It's very important, therefore, to check earnings dates as well as knowing stocks in the same sector. Let's move onto the next rule.

Rule #5 - Trade With the Trend

This is one of my favorite rules, but I find that many traders have a tough time sticking with it. Sticking with the trend is always in your best interest. I am going to share with you how easily we can determine the trend using our favorite exponential moving average. Trading on the right side of the trend will increase your odds significantly. Most people are under the impression that a day trader should focus on a one-minute chart. After all, this is a short-term trade and we should focus on a short-term chart, right? This is false. If you trade on a one-minute chart, odds are you will get shaken out of your trade every minute.

We need to focus on the bigger picture to increase our success rate on a shorter-term trade. We focus on the daily chart to find the trend.

We use a specific exponential moving average called the 8 EMA. This is the moving average looking at the prior eight days, with more weight applied to the most recent days. We call it the 8 train. When stocks are trading above the 8 EMA on the daily chart, they have bullish momentum. We want to ride these stocks up the track. When stocks are trading below the 8 EMA on the daily chart, they have bearish momentum. We want to ride these stocks down the track.

Look at this daily chart of Bank of America (**BAC**):

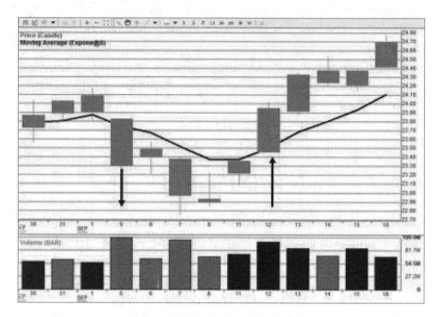

The black line running across the chart is the 8-day exponential moving average (8 EMA). On September 5, 2017, **BAC** closed below the 8 EMA on high volume. That is very bearish. As a day trader we want to go short **BAC** when it's below the 8 EMA. To take a bullish day trade is to go countertrend, and that is a more difficult trade.

On September 12, **BAC** closed above the 8 EMA on high volume. That is very bullish. As a day trader this is when we want to buy it and go long **BAC,** above the 8 EMA.

On September 13, 2017, **BAC** was a perfect Whisper trade. It had over 100K shares in premarket trading volume. It had a penny spread, and was priced below $40. **BAC** was trading above the 8 EMA on the daily chart which gave it a bullish trend. I whispered to buy it above $24.

Here is the 5-minute chart showing great Pre-Market volume:

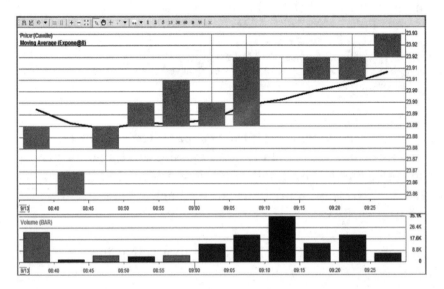

You can see that **BAC** was very active the hour before the market opened, and trading in an upward trend, making higher highs. This is the key to picking the Whisper of the Day: premarket momentum at its best.

The Whisper looked like this:

You can watch this Whisper of the Day:
https://www.youtube.com/watch?v=ldg9ASIxzBw

This is my post from my live trading room that morning. I post up the Whisper levels in the announcement tab.

08:52 **Stefanie Kammerman**: Today\'s Whisper $UUP Bullish above 24 bearish below 23.80: GLD bullish above 126.10 (300K print yesterday) USO bullish above 10: BAC bullish above 23.71 (massive prints yesterday) next entry level bullish above 24

I didn't even tell you about the best part. The previous day, on September 12, we had spotted massive Dark Pool prints on **BAC**. These Dark Pool prints were priced at $23.71 and $23.72. This was highly unusual. We knew a big move was coming on **BAC**.

Here is my post on StockTwits about those big prints.

The_Stock_Whisperer   Sep. 12 at 10:43 AM
The Java Pit Trading Room

Massive prints **$BAC** 2.5 mil $23.73 Bullish above 23.80 Bearish below 23.60

There are the levels. **Bullish above, Bearish below. No thinking!**

If BAC stayed above $23.80, we were bullish. If **BAC** were to close below 23.60 we would have turned bearish. No thinking!

Here is a picture of those big trades off my LIVEVOL® Pro platform. I scanned for all trades over 500K that day. The big trades happened from 10:35am to 10:45am.

There is a lot of intraday noise. Stocks will bounce around quite a lot.

9/12/2017
Hi: 24.03
Lo: 23.45
O: 23.46
C: 23.95
V: 99,658,489
23.8099
AVG:23.501

As an overnight swing trader, I need my stocks to close strong, above the prints. That is exactly what **BAC** did. The stock closed strong near the high of the day on September 12. The closing price was $23.95, above the price of the Dark Pool prints. Here is a picture of the Open, High, Low, Close (OHLC) from that day. You can see the high was $24.03, the low was $23.45, it opened at $23.46 and it closed at $23.95. It closed above all the big prints which was very bullish.

It just so happens that these prints on **BAC** came a few days before the Fed (the Federal Reserve Board of Governors) was scheduled to meet on a possible interest rate hike. I have been trained to read the tape and ignore the news. Even though I do not analyze the news, I am fully aware that events are occurring. I never want to risk a lot of money on these kinds of trades. Small risk, huge reward, lottery ticket trades are best. Risking a little to make a LOT is always best!

Here is my post from the trading room that day announcing my trade and entry into **BAC**. I find the best way to educate my traders is to show them in real time how to enter and exit. Here is the chat log from that day.

10:55 **SuzieQ.** : someone knows if they raise rates or not wish they would share lol
10:55 **Wall_St_Wiz .** : good jobs reports this am.. leans to rate increase
10:56 **SuzieQ.**: lol you the mole
10:56 **Stefanie Kammerman** : B 25 lottto calls on BAC next weeks .04 just in case ;-)
10:56 **Wall_St_Wiz .** : lol
10:56 **Stefanie Kammerman** : you figured it out Suzie
10:56 **Verminator .** : BAC long...risky

At 10:56am, I wrote that I bought the $25 strike calls on **BAC** using the following week's expiration. I paid only four cents for them. The most I could lose on a long basic option is the price I pay for it, in this case four cents. Catching the option chain off guard by following the huge prints on the stock is our secret. Using options as a vehicle with which to trade off the Dark Pool prints allows us to put on low risk trades with minimum capital for potential big gains.

The next day, September 14, **BAC** opened and traded higher immediately. An hour after the open it started to make lower lows. This is where we'll start to scale out of our trades. Here is a look at the 5-minute chart that day:

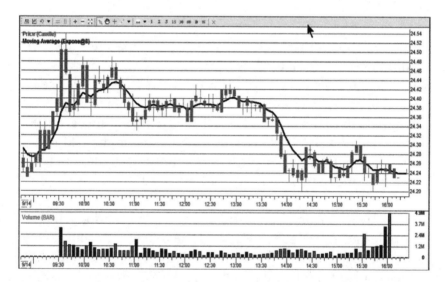

At 10:23am, I announced in our trading room that I was scaling out of a quarter of my position making 80 percent return on investment (ROI).

> **10:23 Stefanie Kammerman**: Out 1/4 BAC 25 calls 80% ROI

After another hour, **BAC** continued to make a lower low so I scaled out of another quarter of my position, making 70 percent ROI.

11:35 **Stefanie Kammerman**: Out another 1/4 BAC calls 70% ROI

As the day progressed, **BAC** continued moving lower so I scaled out of another quarter of my trade making 25 percent ROI.

13:40 **Stefanie Kammerman**: Out another 1/4 BAC calls 25% ROI

I've learned throughout the years to hold onto the last quarter for breakeven or high-end target. In this case it was the high-end target.

15:59 **Stefanie Kammerman**: I'm holding last 1/4 Paul to prevent exit-itis lol

BAC moved much higher over the next week. Look at the daily chart:

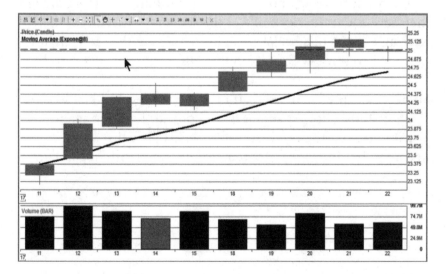

As you can see, following the Dark Pool and following the trend is going to increase your success rate.

We still have a few more important rules to go over. I touched slightly on the levels, but now it's time to go into more detail on them.

Rule #6 - Know Your Levels

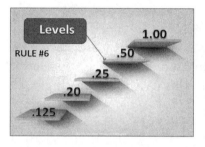

We're trading against computers now. There are no market makers. Nobody is left on the floor of the New York Stock Exchange. Just a room of high frequency computers trying to get the fastest fills.

I have uncovered the best levels off which computers trade. Did you know they trade off the eighth-levels? I discovered this secret in 2009; my biggest "aha" moment of my career. I had just gotten this new trading software. I was zooming in and out of my daily chart when I noticed it. The computers were giving me their levels. On the right side of the screen I noticed that there were all eighths of a dollar lined up. These are the same eighths that I use to trade with back in the '90s.

Some stocks prefer to trade off these eighth levels, like the example I just showed you of **BAC**. Look at the chart again. You'll notice on the right side of the chart. The prices are in decimals, but they are in increments of one-eighth of a dollar.

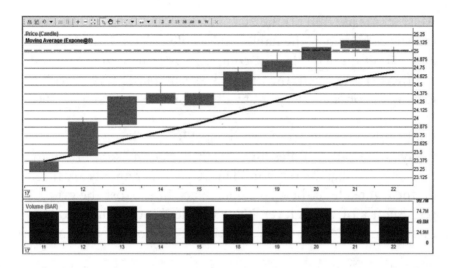

The highs on September 20 and 21 were $25.25, otherwise known as 25 and one-quarter. You can also note that many of the other candles line up perfectly on these eighth-levels. Other stocks prefer more the decimal levels, in 20 cent increments, or one-fifth of a dollar. Look at this next chart of Delta Airlines (**DAL**).

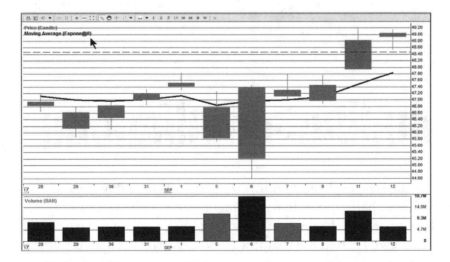

The high of the day on August 29 is $46.80. The high of the day on September 7 is $47.80. The high on September 11 is $49.20. Some stocks prefer the eighths, while other stocks prefer to trade off the fifths levels.

All stocks trade well off the 50 cent and dollar increment levels, otherwise known as the halves and whole dollars. I love to enter and exit off these levels. The computers are lined up to buy and sell there. I love to cut the line and get out a little early. I will exit at .47, for example, just shy of .50, or at .97 just shy of 1.00.

Look at this daily chart of Facebook (**FB**). You'll see that so many of the daily candles hit resistance or found support on the 50 cent- or dollar-increments. The 50 cent increments are listed on the right side of the chart. Each black line across the grid represents a fifty cent level. Many candles hit these half-dollar increment levels with either the wick or the body of the candle.

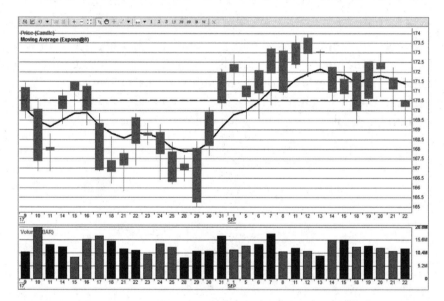

The highest probability of making 20 cents on a day trade is off these half- and dollar-increment levels. This is one of my biggest secrets. I remember teaching this to one of my students years ago. He told me that it was too easy. He was apparently looking for a more complex way to trade. He couldn't fathom that we were trading against computers and these computers were giving us the levels on the right side of our charts. All we had to do was look.

Trading should be purely mathematical. All we need is the right formula.

Here is my formula for putting the odds in your favor:

DAY TRADING
Only Risking .04 to make .20 or more

Day trading Formula

$$\frac{(+100K \text{ volume PM})(\text{Entry at major level})(\text{trend})(\text{dark pool})}{(.04 \text{ stop loss / target exit})} = \text{Successful trade}$$

When we discuss and set up trades in my trading room, we rely on this formula!

Rule #7 - Know Your Exit Strategy

Every day, there will be at least one trader who will ask me if and/or where he or she should get out of the trade. You must always be prepared. You must map out your stop loss and your target exit before you get into your trade. Traders who don't do this will most likely exit their trade for a big loss because fear or greed is controlling them rather than their trading plan.

Would you hop on a plane without having a destination? That's what you're doing when you enter a trade without an exit strategy. I suggest that you only risk four to five cents on each trade and always take 20 cents off the table when the market gives it to you.

You can scale out and try to grab 50 cents or more if the stock warrants that big of move. If your stock moves at least a dollar a day, you can expect to make 50 cents on a trade. If your stock typically moves only 50 cents in a day, you shouldn't expect to grab the entire 50 cents. You would have to enter at the exact low of the day and exit at the exact high of the day. I think getting hit with lightening has a higher probability. Just grab the meat off the trade.

I teach my traders to use the 8 EMA on the 5-minute chart to help exit the trade. If you are long the stock, wait until the first 5-minute candle closes below the 8 EMA before you exit the trade. Sometimes you can ride that 8 train up the hill all day long.

Here is an example of another one of my Whispers: the Energy Select Sector SPDR ETF (**XLE**).

We had huge Dark Pool prints on **XLE** on September 19, 2017, at $66.80. The next day, I whispered that I was bullish on **XLE** above $67. I've drawn a line where the $67 level is on the 5-minute chart.

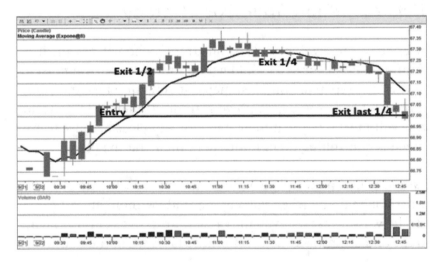

XLE broke above $67 at the perfect time of day to enter a daytrade: 9:50am. Then, **XLE** rode the 8 train beautifully for the next hour. It did not close below the 8 EMA until 11:20am. Scaling out of half a position at $67.20, taking a 20-cent profit off the table immediately is a great trade. You should exit the next quarter position at $67.30 or on a break below the 8

EMA. The last quarter should be either break-even or a target exit at the next major half-dollar level, in this case, at $67.50. In this particular trade, our last quarter was at break-even. Remember scaling = happiness. Scaling prevents exit-itis.

All these rules so far have given us high probability trade set-ups, but I like to take it one more step further with this next rule. Adding this increases the probability of a successful trade.

Rule #8 - Watch the Sector

Align with other stocks, ETFs, or indexes to increase your success rate. In other words, this is like comparing apples to apples. The day we spotted those huge prints on **BAC**, we also spotted huge prints on Citibank (**C**), another bank stock. Here is a picture of those prints:

On September 12, at 12:01pm, 400K printed on **C** at $68.91. This was highly unusual. We don't normally get such big trades on **C** in the middle of the day.

Having two big banks with big prints was confirmation of a big move on the entire sector. There are thousands of other examples I can give you, but we have some more rules to cover. My next rule is all about timing.

Rule #9 - It's All About Timing

The second test. The second time around is always better than the first when it comes to entering. The first time a stock hits a major resistance level, all the computers are lined up to sell there. Your stock might go over that level by a few pennies, sometimes a little more, but 95 percent of the time, the stock will pull back. Depending upon the stock, it can pull back quite a bit. You should always sell into strength by cutting the line before that resistance level. For example, if your target is at $163.00, sell at around $162.86.

If you are going to enter a new trade on the $163 level, make sure you are entering on the second test. The second test should be at least 25 minutes after the first time the stock hit $163. The stock should also have increasing volume coming into it as it is breaking above the level. This tells us that real buying is coming in now to push it above and keep it above that next level.

Look at this next chart of Home Depot (**HD**) on September 29, 2017:

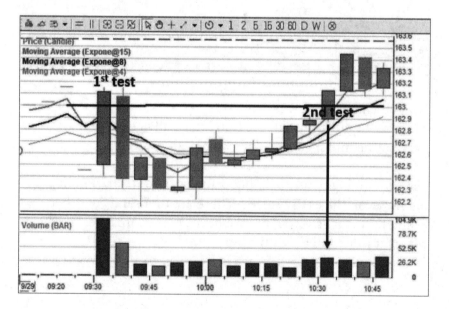

At 9:30am, **HD** tested the $163 level. You can see it went above the level by a few pennies. Note at 10:30am, it retested $163. This second test came at least after 25 minutes after the first test. Note also the increasing volume that came in when it broke above $163 on this retest. This is the best time to enter a day trade.

As a swing trader I like to wait for the second test of a major level on a daily chart.

Here is a daily chart of **HD**, showing August and September of 2017:

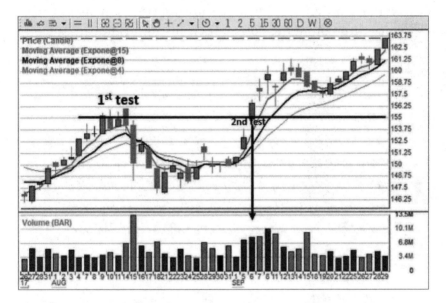

On August 9th, **HD** tested the $155 level for the first time. The $5 increments are the strongest levels, making them ideal for a swing trade entry. I'll go into more detail on these levels in the swing trading chapter. You want to wait for a nice pull back before the second test on high volume before you enter.

On September 2, **HD** finally retested the $155 level on above average volume. This is your best entry on a swing using the second time around rule.

We're almost done. We have one more rule.

Rule #10 - Prints Trump Everything

Prints give us carte blanche to break every single rule we just covered. Big prints trump everything. You can enter a trade at any time if you have a big print. You can go against the trend. The big print becomes the entry level, so you don't have to wait for the stock to be at ideal entries of the half- and dollar-increment levels. Prints take precedence over everything. That's how important they are. I will be showing you so many more examples throughout the book, especially in this next chapter.

> Stefanie's unique approach and energetic style to short-term trading strategies makes intuitive sense and is easy to understand for the average investor. Getting behind the big money flow on a short-term basis means you are trading with deep pockets supporting you rather than against you. This special skill set to trade with the big money traders earned her the nickname the VolumePrintcess. Stefanie is at the top of her game.
>
> Larry Berman
> Founder ETF Capital Management,
> Host of Berman's Call on BNN

Chapter 7

DAY TRADING
BIG PRINTS

Every morning before the market opens, I do a special segment in my trading room called "The Whisper of the Day." The Whisper includes my hottest stock picks. I always post the Whisper in the announcement tab in my room and a few days later it's posted on my YouTube channel for the public.

During our daily Pre-Market morning meeting from 9-9:30am, I go over how to trade these Whispers along with numerous other high-probability trades. I have been doing these Whispers since 2014. My success rate is over 90 percent since I started the Whispers. You can take a listen to several years of Whispers on my YouTube channel. Each video is about three to four minutes long. Here is the link to watch:
www.youtube.com/user/thestockwhisperer

There are literally a hundred amazing trades to take all day long following the big prints. I wish I could take them all, but

I only have two eyes. I try to find the best ones. I trade stocks that I am familiar with. I stay away from biotech stocks because they can get halted at any time. I search for the best trades that have room to run. After you study the tape for a few months, you will notice which trades are highly unusual. Those are the trades you want to take. When you are doing a short-term trade, you do not have time to sit and wait for a stock to move. Having this huge print is almost a guarantee that the stock is going to move. There are days I feel like an ambulance chaser, except I am chasing the smart money. These are the guys that are moving the stock and I want to get in right behind them.

I'm going to walk you through a couple examples of day trades that we did in my Java Pit. One is a straight-forward day trade using options and the other is an overnight swing trade.

Intraday Trading

Remember the Facebook (**FB**) print that I covered in Chapter 3? Here are the quick details:

On July 27, 2017, we spotted a 3.6 million print at $174.28. We were bullish above $175 and bearish below $174. NO thinking!!

Let's look at the day trade we did in my trading room.

At 11:50am, **FB** dropped below $174 and I called out a trade.

> (11:50) **Stefanie K**: B cheap lotto puts on FB exp tomorrow
> (11:51) **Stefanie K**: 172.50/170
> (11:51) **Stefanie K**: maybe Bloomberg had the right earnings lol
> (11:51) **Amit M**: Stef iv is still high
> (11:52) **Amit M**: o FB options
> (11:52) **Wall St Wiz**: nice Stef... I like your plan
> (11:52) **Stefanie K**: it has to really get crushed into tomorrow, or else I lose on this, but it's a small risk

I called out that I was buying cheap lotto puts on **FB** that were expiring the next day. July 27 was a Thursday, which is my favorite day to find cheap options that are expiring the next day. Options with only one day left to expiration have very little remaining time value, so one can often buy these for pennies. Buying these "cheap lotto puts" meant that I was going out of the money, so the only way to make money on these is if **FB** were to have a huge move. The odds were in our favor based on this 3.6 million print.

I went out of the money (OTM) and bought the $172.50 strike puts for 54 cents. I also bought some further out of the money $170 strike puts for 15 cents. Remember **FB** was just trading right under $174 when I entered this trade. We call these far out of the money options plays "lotto trades" for two reasons. One reason is because we risk only what we would risk if we were going to buy a lottery ticket for the Powerball. We don't risk a lot of money in these trades. I don't actually play Powerball because my odds are much better in the market following the Dark Pool. Buying these OTM options off big prints is the only way I like to "play the lotto". The second reason we call these lotto trades is that we enter these trades with the understanding that we may not make money on these trades, much like most lottery tickets. Many of our lotto trades are full risk trades.

Not all my traders shorted **FB** using options. Lesley, aka Glider Girl, shorted the stock at $173.40.

(11:58) **Lesley C**: SS FB 173.40
(11:58) **Verminator**: CMCSA, QQQ AMD all sittin on prints thinking about it.....
(11:58) **Amit M**: but if my market tanks, NVDA can go below 150
(11:59) **Stefanie K**: Dump during lunch, these armani's throw these big prints at us every day at lunch becuase they don't think anybody is watching

I didn't think **FB** was going to dump this fast, but it did. It took the elevator down quite a few floors over the next hour.

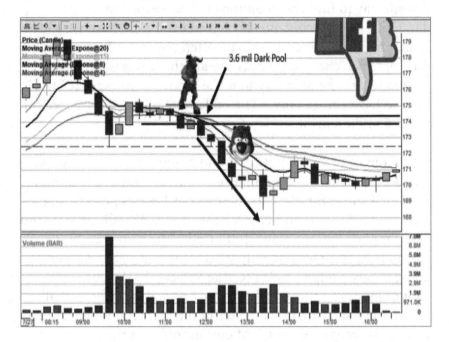

Above is a 15-minute chart from that day. I drew a line at 175 where we were bullish above, and I drew a line at $174 where we were bearish below. Once **FB** broke below $174, it came all the way down to $168. My OTM puts were now in the money (ITM) and worth a lot more.

The same way we shouldn't try to peg the top, I try to not peg the bottom. Over the years, I suffered a terrible trading disease called "Exit-itis," that inflammation of frustration that occurs when you exit out of a trade too quickly. This can occur daily and can lead to extreme unhappiness. Not only did I suffer from exit-itis, so many of my traders also suffered from this horrific disease.

I found a cure from exit-itis. Scaling! Scaling is the cure for exit-itis and leads to happiness. Scaling out of your positions will help you prevent exit-itis. When you take some profit off the table, you immediately feel happy. If your trade continues to make money, you're happy you are still in it. If your trade goes against you, you're happy you took some profit. I will take profit when my options reach 100 percent return on investment (ROI). Let me show you how we do that.

Here is a chat from 16 minutes after I had called out my trade entry:

> (12:06) **Blanca P**: out FB puts +0.11 (81%)
> (12:06) **Stefanie K**: wtg Blanca!!
> (12:07) **Stefanie K**: love big prints on Thursday
> (12:07) **Verminator**: USO above the print
> (12:08) **Stefanie K**: out of half FB 172.50 puts 100% ROI

One of my traders, Blanca, made 81 percent ROI in less than 20 minutes. I exited out of half of my $172.50 strike puts for 100 percent ROI.

> (12:21) **Stefanie K**: out another 1/5 172.50 puts FB 200% ROI

I exited some more of my $172.50 strike puts for 200 percent ROI.

> (12:24) **Stefanie K**: out of half 170 FB puts 275% sold for .41
> (12:24) **Ricki B**: good job Amit
> (12:24) **Blanca P**: nice Stef!

I was scaling out into strength, which is a great exit strategy to use with options. The best option traders in our trading room are great day traders.

> (12:44) **Stefanie K**: out another 1/4 FB 170's 1.19
> (12:44) **Stefanie K**: wow

On this fourth of my $170 strike puts position, I made over 600 percent ROI in just one hour. Total on this **FB** trade, I made over 100 percent ROI on my $172.50 strike puts, and my $170 strike puts netted me over 350 percent ROI.

> (13:34) **David T**: out 1/2 FB daytrade puts 400%

> (13:59) **Lesley C**: out shorts WB +.2.63, WYNN 2.37, LABD +.31, FB +2.32
> (13:59) **Blanca P**: wow Lesley
> (13:59) **Cowboy**: Nice tradin Lesley

Lesley did very nicely trading the stock off that Dark Pool **FB** print. David also did very well trading options. You can see how those of us who used options as a vehicle with which to trade the stock really capitalized on the leverage that these options provide. Whether we trade stock or options, this is how we day trade using the Dark Pool prints.

Overnight Swing Trading

I've trained my traders to call out all the unusual prints throughout the day and they do a great job. Everybody asks me why I do this. Why do I train thousands of traders to look for these huge unusual prints? The answer is simple, "This way, I don't have to work so hard anymore!"

General Chat Transcript

Room Name: Java Pit
Date and Time: February 12 2018 06:30:12

On February 12, 2018 Gerald called out a print on Nuance Communications Inc. (**NUAN**):

(14:34)   **Gerald N**: NUAN 16, 3.3 M

Just in case you missed Gerald's call out, Lorraine called it out a minute later.

(14:35)   **Lorraine B**: big p NUAN @ 16 3.38 mil

Here is a picture of the print in LIVEVOL® Pro:

Time ▲	Symbol	Qty	Price
14:34:04	NUAN	3386300	16.0000
14:39:03	NUAN	1000000	16.0000

You can see a few minutes later we got another print. A million shares printed at the same level $16. Somebody was hot for **NUAN**.

As soon as I get these huge prints, I always send out notifications to my followers. Here is what I tweeted and posted up in our announcement tab in our live trading room.

2/12/2018   Massive 3 mil print $NUAN $16.00 Bullish above $16.25, Bearish
2:47:12 PM   below $15.75

These huge prints create big splashes. It's best to wait a few hours before jumping in.

Being that it was near the end of the day, I waited until the following day February 13th to swing **NUAN** overnight. We spot over a hundred overnight swing trade opportunities like this every week. The next morning, I put this trade set up in my Whisper of the Day video.

2/13/2018 8:55:49 AM	Todays Whisper $SPY levels $264.46, $262.85, $265.49: $NUAN 3 mil print $16, bullish above $16.25, Bearish below $15.80: $XT 10 mil print, $35.64 Bullish above 36, bearish below 35.50: $NANR 9 mil print 33.41, bullish above 34, bearish below 33: $XLF 5 mil $28.15, bullish above 28.35, bearish below 27.75: SIVR Bullish above 16.25, video out shortly

2/13/2018 9:15:55 AM	Todays Whisper https://www.youtube.com/watch?v=oTOsFEhFN_U&feature-youtu.be

Here is what I called out in my room when I entered the trade. I waited until the end of the day, the last 30 minutes, making sure that **NUAN** closed above the prints.

This trade broke a few of my rules. The first rule is it didn't close above the 8 EMA on the daily chart. The 2nd rule it broke was that it didn't close on above average volume, or greater volume than the day before. I will break all my rules if I have a huge unusual print. That is how powerful the prints are. This is exactly what happened. The fact that it closed above $16 allowed me to get into the trade following my rules.

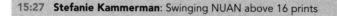

15:27 Stefanie Kammerman: Swinging NUAN above 16 prints

Below is the High, Low, Open, Close (OHLC) on **NUAN** from February 13th, 2018 along with the daily chart. I have drawn an arrow to where it closed at $16.11 as well as a circle on the daily chart.

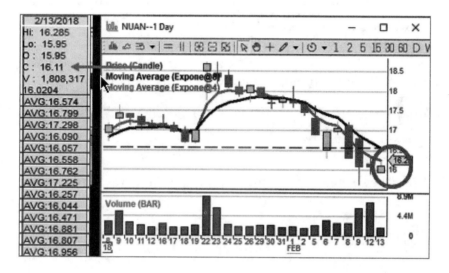

Normally I would trade the options, because the risk is much lower, but the options didn't look great. I did not see adequate volume on them and they had a huge spread.

The fact that **NUAN** was inexpensively priced at $16, I opted to buy the stock.

I could not pass up this trade. It does not matter what you trade with using this system. Trade what you feel comfortable with. I like to keep my risk as low as possible knowing a big move is going to happen so catching the options chain off guard by buying them cheap is my preferred method.

Stevan was confused and asked me what my trade was, expecting that I did an options trade.

15:30   **Stevan .** : Stef - What's your trade on NUAN?

I always call out what strike and expiration I do with options. I told him I did not like the options.

15:30   **Stefanie Kammerman**: the stock Stevan, no options
15:31   **Stefanie Kammerman**: they aren't good

He asked me my thoughts on the March 17 call options.

15:32   **Stevan .** : Nuan - What about the MAR 17s?

I said they weren't bad, some volume, but there was a .10 spread.

15:33   **Stefanie Kammerman** : not bad Stevan, some volume on those, but .
10 spread

Over the next 2 days **NUAN** started to move up. That 8 EMA is like a brick wall, so I like to scale out and take some profits on it.

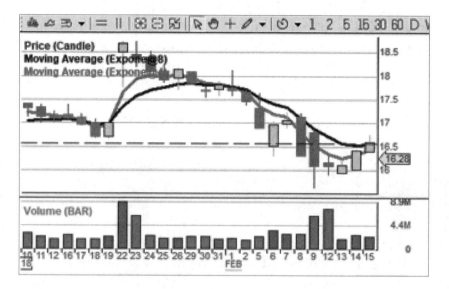

Here is what we posted up in our trading room on February 15th, 2018:

General Chat Transcript

Room Name: Java Pit
Date and Time: February 15 2018 06:50:01

Apparently, I was not the only one to hop into this trade. A new trader Michael announced he was in it too. He wanted to know my thoughts on his exit strategy.

> 09:25 **Michael O** : long Nuan from 16.16 yesterday looking to exit 16.75 around 200 sma. any thoughts ??

I answered his question during my daily morning meeting

which is from 9:00-9:30 am. I review all the highest probability day trade setups along with whatever stocks my traders in my room would like me to comment on. One of the most popular requests I get is to see if there are any unusual prints on their stocks. I will also draw trend lines and look up on my ECN (Electronic Communications Network) book to see where the big traders are buying and selling. This is my little black book. This is where all the big guys hide their orders.

David called out that there was news on **NUAN**.

> 09:28 **David C** : NUAN news yesterday https://drive.google.com/open?id=1g-JE4bF7eJdJrw7R4QXmfji-ucU-xbWB said "Receives 20.50 price target from brokerages"

It turns out that they received a $20.50 price target from brokerages. The prints always come first, way before the news. Therefore, we want to trade off the prints and sell into the news.

I took some profit after hearing the news and scaled out of half. Michael also took some profit.

> 09:35 **Michael O** : out of nuan 16.50 up .34 on trade .
> 09:35 **Sharkman .** : Hitting 56.50 level
> 09:35 **Blanca Perez** : XOP testing prints
> 09:35 **Stefanie Kammerman** : Out of half NUAN 16.43 +.24

I announced that my target was around $16.80. Stevan called out that it was above the 8 EMA.

Prints came first again.

> 09:52 **Stefanie Kammerman** : 16.80 next target for NUAN
> 09:53 **Stevan .** : NUAN -- above the 8ema

I scaled out of another ¼ of my position at my target near the end of the day.

> **15:19** **Stefanie Kammerman** : out another 1/4 NUAN 2nd target +.50 off the 3 million prints at 16 from the other day

Apparently, I was not the only one who made good money on **NUAN**. A new trader named Witold who I met at the Orlando MoneyShow the week before joined my room and had a great week.

> **16:01** **Witold O** : Thanks again Stef. I sold my SPY, AAPL, IWD & NUAN. Portfolio now up 20.5% since Monday

The next day I exited out of my last ¼ on **NUAN**. It was having a tough time and approaching the 50 SMA.

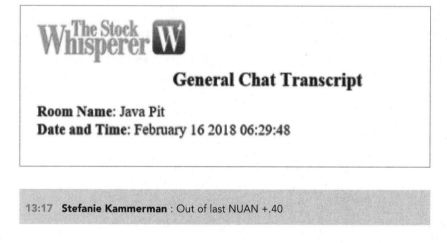

The Stock WHISPERER W

General Chat Transcript

Room Name: Java Pit
Date and Time: February 16 2018 06:29:48

> **13:17** **Stefanie Kammerman** : Out of last NUAN +.40

Stevan exited out of his **NUAN** calls making 50 percent ROI.

> **13:20** **Stevan** : NUAN - Sold calls paid .30 got .45 +50%

You can see we did well on this trade!

NUAN hit the 200 SMA and started to come down again. That is a very powerful moving average. Therefore, you want to exit here. If it were too close above, you can take another swing at it.

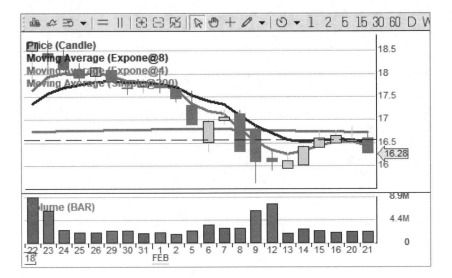

Now we will wait for it to retest that $16 level. If it holds, we will go long again. If it does not hold, that would be bearish. Always stay on the right side of the prints.

> *The Stock Whisperer lives up to her name. Over the years of interviewing Stefanie I have been amazed at how spot on she is when it comes to calling the next move in the market. She is a must follow for all traders.*
>
> *Matthew D. McCall*
> *President, Penn Financial Group*

Chapter 8

SWING TRADING BIG PRINTS

Everybody always assumes that I am just a day trader. I prefer to swing trade, but since I am watching the tape all day, I might as well do a few day trades. I think that swing trading is where the big money is to be made. Following the big prints will give you a huge edge. I like to combine that with momentum. You want everything working in your favor. You don't want any roadblocks or traffic lights in front of you.

In this chapter, I will show you a few examples of how I combine the prints, my favorite moving averages, the 4 and 8 EMA to determine the trend, as well as seasonality to really increase our success rate. It is great to have a few tools in your tool box and these are my secret tools.

Swing Trading Using the 8-Day EMA

In Chapter 6, I introduced you to the 8-day exponential moving average (8 EMA). We call it the 8 train. This is just one of the tools I use to determine trend changes.

On October 26, 2016, at 10:03am, we spotted the biggest prints we had ever seen on Hewlett Packard (**HPQ**). Five million share printed at $13.90. Here are those trades on my LIVEVOL® Pro software:

Time ▲	Symbol	Qty	Price	Exchange	Condition	Market
10:03:31	HPQ	1900000	13.9000	NQNX	Regular	13.89 x 13.9
10:03:31	HPQ	1200000	13.9000	NQNX	Regular	13.89 x 13.9
10:03:31	HPQ	1900000	13.9000	NQNX	Regular	13.89 x 13.9

Karl, aka Santa, called it out in the trading room first. At 10:05am, he typed this chat.

> **10:05** **Santa** : HPQ P13.90 5.0m daily sitting on 120sma

He also noted that it was sitting on the 120-day simple moving average (SMA). That is a very powerful moving average. If you don't have that on your daily chart, I highly suggest you put it on ASAP. Trust me, you'll love it! Ricki, the Options Whisperer, suggested that we put it on our charts a few years back. It is so powerful at being a support and resistance level that my traders joke about it, asking me if I can take it off the chart so that their stocks can move. In this case, **HPQ** was sitting on the 120-day SMA as support.

Wayne, another one of my traders, we call him the Cowboy, jumped into some **HPQ** calls. He put on a "lottery ticket trade", buying inexpensive calls stating it looked like buying. Here are his call outs in the trading room:

> 10:32 **Cowboy** : NSFW - bot HPQ lottery C's 13.89

> 10:37 **Cowboy** : HPQ those 13.90 -5M prints look like buy

NSFW means Not Safe For Work. It means, "kids, do not try this at home." Follow me only if you know what you are doing.

For me, it looked like a no-brainer. These calls were so cheap, the risk was so small, and the reward was so high. I loved it so much I put it into my Whisper of the Day the next day, on October 27, 2016. You can listen to this Whisper on my YouTube page.

Here is what I posted up in our trading room:

> 08:40 **Stefanie Kammerman** : Today's Whisper " Still bearish on gold below those prints, GT 29 , bullish above, bearish below: USO bearish below 11.12: HPQ bullish above 13.90, bearish below

That morning, **HPQ** went straight up from the open. Here is the chat from that morning:

> 09:41 **Thomas** : HPQ straight up from the open.
> 09:42 **Stefanie Kammerman** : /ES stuck in a tight spot there Ron
> 09:42 **Foxy_Roxy .** : b CRUS
> 09:42 **Wall_St_Wiz .** : yup Stef..
> 09:43 **Cathy .** : Wow HPQ
> 09:44 **Stefanie Kammerman** : HPQ needs to break above the 8ema on daily chart, it's a brick wall

Even though we had those massive five million share prints, I still wanted to see **HPQ** break above the 8 EMA on the daily chart. That would be bullish confirmation.

At the end of day, **HPQ** closed above $13.90 but below the 8 EMA. In my afternoon meeting that day, I announced that I was buying some cheap calls for 15 cents.

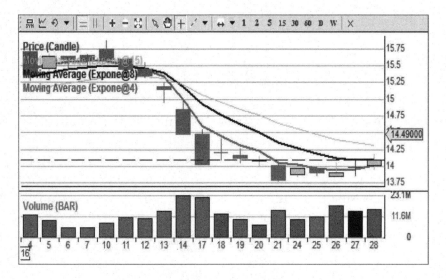

You can see that **HPQ** tried to break above the 8 EMA, but it hit it like a brick wall. It closed as a high volume doji. A doji candle is an indecision candle. It closes exactly where it opened. It's a tug of war between the bulls and the bears. It's one of my favorite candles when it happens on above average volume. We know a big move is about to happen. If **HPQ** closes above the high of that candle within the next few days, that will be extremely bullish. If it closes below the low of that candle, that will be very bearish. Let's look at the Open, High, Low, Close (OHLC) for that day:

10/27/2016
Hi: 14.095
Lo: 13.87
O : 13.99
C : 13.99
V : 14,106,496
13.9266
AVG:14.462
AVG:14.350
AVG:14.094
AVG:13.965

You can see from the OHLC that **HPQ** rallied up to a high of $14.09 before retracing and closing at $13.99. As long as **HPQ** remains and closes above $13.90, the print level, we will continue to be bullish; however, a close above $13.99 (the doji close) would be more bullish, and a close above $14.10 (above the high of the doji) would be uber bullish.

Guess what happened the next day? You're not going to believe this, but we got more prints on **HPQ**. Another 2.8 million shares printed at the same price of $13.90. There was a computer loaded to buy as much as possible at that price. Every time **HPQ** tested that price, it bounced off it. Let me show you these fresh set of prints:

Time ▲	Symbol	Qty	Price	Exchange	Condition	Market
10:14:28	HPQ	840062	13.9000	NQNX	IntermarketSweep	13.88 x 13.89
10:17:34	HPQ	1000000	13.9000	NQNX	Regular	13.89 x 13.9
10:21:54	HPQ	1000000	13.9000	NQNX	Regular	13.9 x 13.91

Ten minutes later, at 10:34am, I added onto my **HPQ** calls.

> **10:34 Stefanie Kammerman** : Added another 1/4 HPQ long swing

Santa announced that **HPQ** was crossing above the 8 EMA.

> **11:25 Santa .** : HPQ ww crossing 8ema

At 12:09pm, I took some profit on **HPQ**.

> **12:09 Stefanie Kammerman** : Out of 1/4 HPQ +.20

I exited out of a fourth of my original position, grabbing 20 cents profit. I told the Cowboy that I was still holding some calls that I had bought for 15 cents.

> **12:12 Stefanie Kammerman** : Still in those HPQ calls for .15 cowboy

The next day, October 28, **HPQ** moved up. Can you guess where it closed?

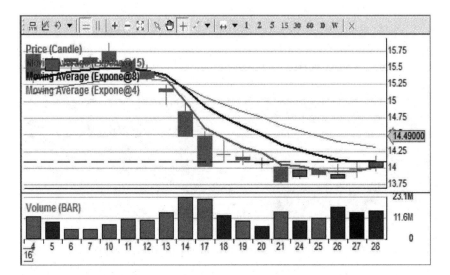

It closed right on $14.09. That was the high of that high volume doji candle on October 27. We were still bullish because we were above the prints, and so we held onto our call options for a swing.

On October 31, the following Monday, as **HPQ** continued to move up, I whispered again. This time I was bullish above $14.20. Here is what I posted up in my trading room that morning:

[08:36] **Stefanie Kammerman** : Today's Whisper MU bullish above 17.75 bearish below 17.60: HPQ still like it, bullish above 14.20: USO still bearish , if it can't hold 10.87 , next level down is 10.75

I posted that I still liked **HPQ**, bullish above 14.20. Many of my traders in my room were jumping into **HPQ** with me.

Here are their live chats:

Vernon bought **HPQ**.

[12:33] **Vernon** : ill be back...in HPQ long....hope is doesnt run away...;>

At 1:12pm, I took some more profits by selling another fourth of my original position.

[13:12] **Stefanie Kammerman** : Out another 1/4 HPQ 14.30+.29

I then took some more profit on my calls 27 minutes later, at 1:39pm.

[13:39] **Stefanie Kammerman** : Out of 1/4 HPQ calls +.26, paid .15 for them 80% ROI

Daniel made 100 percent ROI on his calls.

[14:16] **Daniel** : out of HPQ Calls +100% thanks coach!

Vernon scaled out making 17 cents on his trade.

[14:54] **Vernon** : scale HPQ .17

[15:44] **Stefanie Kammerman** : out of another 1/4 HPQ calls .36 150% ROI

I scaled out the last quarter of my original position at 3:44pm, making 150 percent ROI.

Scaling = Happiness

Let me show you a chart of what **HPQ** did that day:

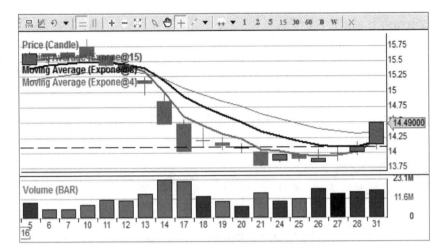

HPQ finally moved up, closing above those important levels. Our target on **HPQ** was $15. That was the next strongest swing level up. On November 1, many of the traders took their profits.

[10:25] **Yin T** : out HPQ +0.19

The Cowboy made 400 percent ROI on his calls.

[09:40] **Cowboy** : out last HPQ C's 14.50 +400%
[09:40] **Pink Panther** : Yippee I O CB
[09:40] **Stefanie K** : wooooo hooooo Cowboy
[09:40] **Cathy** : Wow CB! awesome!
[09:40] **Stefanie K** : you rocked that
[09:40] **Cowboy** : thx, nice call Coach

Tdog made 52 cents on his **HPQ** stock swing. Not everybody trades options in my room. Some traders prefer to trade the stock.

[09:36] **Tdog** : HPQ out swing +0.52
[09:36] **Cowboy** : gj Tdog

I held onto my last quarter, that quarter that I had added on after seeing the additional prints, as long as I could. On November 7, I exited out of the last of my position. Below is the chat from that day:

At 11:48am, I exited out of my final **HPQ** calls, making 450 percent ROI.

[11:48] **Stefanie Kammerman** : Out of my last 1/4 HPQ +.70 14.50 calls 450% ROI of course on my last 1/4
[11:48] **Stefanie Kammerman** : thank you cathy for calling that out
[11:48] **SuzieQ .** : wow stef great trade
[11:48] **Viking_John .** : wow! Stef real nice!!
[11:48] **ricki b** : sweet Stef ... excellent job!

Before you get too excited about my trade, look what **HPQ** did after I got out. It went all the way to $16. I'm not going to lie and tell you I didn't suffer from a little exit-itis. Earnings came out on November 23, and it dropped back down to $15. That cured my exit-itis very quickly.

I have learned never to hold stocks into earnings. It is gambling. Sometimes you can get lucky, but most times you are unlucky. Trading shouldn't be about luck.

Here is the daily chart of **HPQ**. We didn't try to peg the top. We got the meat of the trade – the highest probability trade, using options as a vehicle.

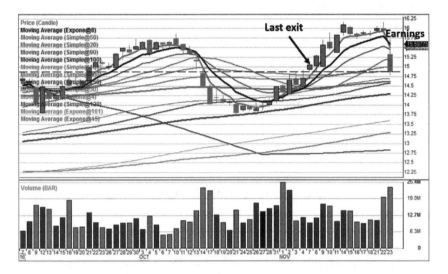

Swing Trading Using the 4 & 8 EMA Crossover

I like to combine the 8 EMA with the 4 EMA. We have already discussed that the weekly chart is the strongest chart for bigger moves.

Here is a simple way to observe when a trend change is happening. A trend change usually occurs when the 4 EMA crosses above or below the 8 EMA on your chart. Sometimes these two moving averages come together before separating again. We need to see an actual crossover. In addition to the crossover, we also need to see volume. Volume is always the key to a higher success rate on any strategy we use.

Let me show you a picture of when the trend doesn't change. Here is the weekly chart of the **SPY** from January 2017 until November 2017:

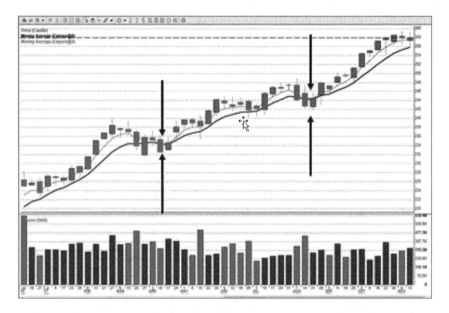

The 4 EMA is the lighter dotted line and the 8 EMA is the solid black line. I've drawn arrows where on two occasions, April and August, the 4 EMA came down to the 8 EMA, touched it and bounced back up again. This is bullish positive long-term momentum. The 4 EMA has higher velocity than the 8 EMA. We call the 4 EMA the express train. Stocks or ETFs that trade on it are moving much faster than stocks that are riding the 8 train.

One of the most popular questions my students ask me is, "When can I break the trend rule?" They think or feel the market is toppy or has found a bottom, and they want to jump in early. They want to get in at the very beginning of a trend change, but the trend hasn't changed yet.

My answer is always the same, "Show me the prints." Show me that the big guys are selling at the top or buying at the bottom. Trust me, we see this every time. The only time you should go against the trend is when you see a huge print. My rebellious students love this rule because it gives them carte blanche to break all my rules. Prints trump everything. That's how powerful they are.

Here is a chart on iShares Gold Trust (**IAU**) where there are many trend changes and you can see the 4 EMA crosses above and below the 8 EMA:

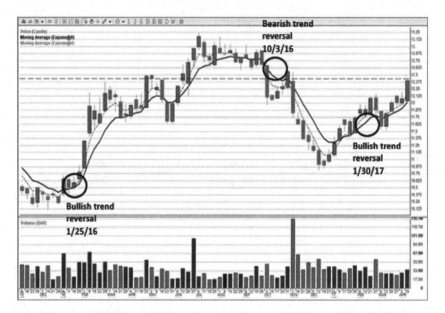

For those of you who like to trade gold, you must watch **IAU**. This is the Dark Pool favorite. Let's start with the crossovers first.

On this weekly chart of **IAU**, you can see that the 4 EMA crossed over the 8 EMA on January 25, 2016. The trend changed from bearish to bullish until the 4 EMA crossed below the 8 EMA on October 3, 2016. Gold made lower lows until the trend changed on January 30, 2017 when the 4 EMA crossed back above the 8 EMA.

Let me give you a brief history on gold before we dive deep into the Dark Pool prints. Gold prices had a huge rally starting from

2009 where it made a dramatic move up from $700 an ounce to $1,923 an ounce into 2011. After peaking out, unable to make higher highs, the trend changed. Gold turned extremely bearish from 2013 until 2016. It took a huge dive down making lower lows until it came down to $1,045 an ounce. Every rally it had was overcome with sellers. Traders started to hate gold, and who could blame them? Many of the traders I talked to wrote gold off. They refused to trade it anymore. The chart looked ugly.

Here is the gold futures, **/GC**, chart going from 2010 until 2017:

In 2011, **/GC** peaked at 1923.7. Then, after **/GC** broke the major support line around $1,525 an ounce, it came rolling down the hill for the next 3 years. What happened when it hit $1,045 an ounce? Why did it stop? Why was that the bottom? I'll give you a hint. It has something to do with the Dark Pool.

I spotted the most massive prints I have ever seen on **IAU**. As soon as I spotted them, I had to tweet and let everybody know that buyers were finally coming in to save gold. Here is my tweet from January 25, 2016 on StockTwits:

The_Stock_Whisperer   Jan. 25 at 12:18 PM
The Java Pit Trading Room

BIG print alert $IAU over 10 million @ 10.70 bullish above, bearish below, no thinking!

On January 25, just after noon, I spotted two blocks of five million prints that came in on **IAU** at $10.70. Let me show you the actual prints from my LIVEVOL˙ Pro software:

Time ▲	Symbol	Qty	Price
12:01:40	IAU	5000000	10.7019
12:02:02	IAU	5880668	10.7019

Note on the last chart of **IAU** that I showed, the 4 EMA crossed above the 8 EMA on January 25, 2016. The same exact time this crossover happened, we got these huge buy prints. I love when these things line up perfectly.

Guess what we spotted next? More prints! We got more buying that was coming in on **IAU** on February 2nd at 12:40pm ET. The Dark Pool loves to buy during lunch. Schonfeld Securities use to buy us lunch every day. Every morning we filled out our lunch ticket. At 12pm they delivered our lunches right to our desk. Schonfeld didn't want us leaving our desk and missing any of these amazing trades.

Here is my tweet after spotting another 10 million shares on **IAU** at $10.85:

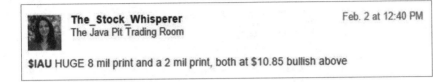

The_Stock_Whisperer
The Java Pit Trading Room

Feb. 2 at 12:40 PM

$IAU HUGE 8 mil print and a 2 mil print, both at $10.85 bullish above

Here is the picture of those actual prints on my LIVEVOL® Pro software:

Individual option trades

Select or Input   IAU Feb19'16 1 P (0)

IAU IAU Feb19'16 1 P 02/02/2016

Underlying trades

Time ▲	Symbol	Qty	Price
12:34:26	IAU	2000000	10.8500
12:37:45	IAU	8782514	10.8500

I felt it was my job to inform all these gold hating traders that the gold hibernation was finally over. Below is just one of my many tweets that I had sent out:

The_Stock_Whisperer
@Cousin_Vinny The $GOLD hibernation is over, a lot more room to run

Feb. 5 at 8:00 PM

You must understand that every small gold rally that we had over the past few years was knocked down, so traders were very hesitant to jump in. I knew that things were very different this time. The Dark Pool was buying in massive amounts. Gold was about to have a stellar move.

I did my best to whisper wherever I went. Being on tour with the MoneyShow and the TradersEXPO around the country was a great way for me to get the word out. I toured from coast to coast and across Canada with Larry Berman. I whispered that gold was going to be the trade of the year.

In an interview by Matt McCall, President of Penn Financial Group, at the Orlando MoneyShow in February 2016, I spoke of these huge prints. I said that we were finally coming out of the gold coma. Here is a picture from that video.

Are We Coming Out of the Gold Coma?

Stefanie Kammerman
Founder, Stock Whisperer Trading Company
MORE ON: COMMODITIES

Released: 4/11/2016
Stefanie Kammerman explains why she currently feels that any significant pullback would be a great opportunity to get into gold.

You can watch the interview here:
https://www.thestockwhisperer.com/Video-Photos/Video-Gallery

The buy prints rallied **IAU's** price from $10.70 up to $13.25. That is a huge move for **IAU**. Most of my traders don't trade **IAU** because they find it to be very slow. They prefer to trade **GLD**, **GDX**, or **ABX**. Some prefer to trade the gold futures. It does not matter what specific instrument you trade. What matters is knowing the direction of where gold is headed. The Dark Pool loves to trade **IAU**, so we follow the prints on **IAU**. **IAU** gives us the direction, but we trade other vehicles.

Let me show you that weekly chart again on **IAU** so you don't have to flip back through pages:

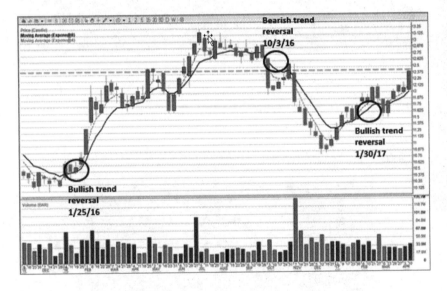

The 4 EMA crossed below the 8 EMA around October 3, 2016. Guess what we spotted? You guessed it right. Prints!

Before the market opened on November 9, 2016, we spotted a huge 8.5 million print on **IAU** at $12.55. This was the first huge print we had spotted since the Dark Pool was buying back in January. Here is a picture of the print:

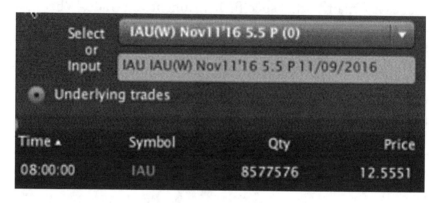

I liked this trade so much I had to put it in my Whisper of the Day video on YouTube from November 9, 2016.

In the Whisper, I talked about this huge print and how we were going to be bullish above, bearish below $12.55. No thinking! **IAU** dropped down quickly, never going above $12.55, so we turned bearish.

The next day, November 10, we spotted more massive sell prints on **IAU** right after the opening bell. I had to tweet that out A.S.A.P.

The_Stock_Whisperer   Nov. 10 at 9:41 AM
The Java Pit Trading Room

HUGE print $IAU 12.24 7 mil Bearish below

Here is a snapshot of those prints.

Time ▲	Symbol	Qty	Price
09:37:15	IAU	7103371	12.2400
10:28:25	IAU	585974	12.2200

Input: IAU IAU(W) Nov11'16 5.5 P 11/10/2016
Underlying trades

As if this wasn't enough, we spotted even more sell prints on November 11. Another eight million printed at $12.09:

Select: IAU(W) Nov11'16 5.5 P (0)
Input: IAU IAU(W) Nov11'16 5.5 P 11/11/2016
Underlying trades

Time ▲	Symbol	Qty	Price
08:00:06	IAU	8000000	12.0914
14:04:18	IAU	1280626	11.7500

My trading room was shorting gold in every way, shape, or form. These were the biggest Dark Pool sell prints we have seen a very long time.

That morning, **IAU** dropped down immediately after the opening bell.

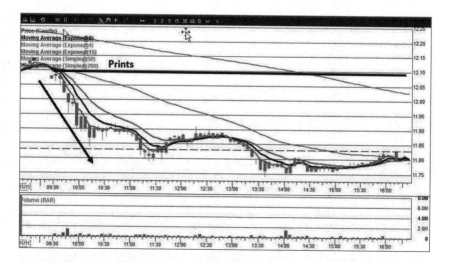

Here is a little excerpt from my trading room that morning:

[09:42] **Stefanie K** : IAU below print, flush away
[09:43] **MoneyPenny** : in DUST @ 46.51 stopped out @ 46.75 = +0.24
[09:43] **Gopi S** : b JDST 33.79
[09:44] **Cameron O** : next stop 22.00 for GDX today and then 20.00 ultimately
[09:44] **Pinky Panther** : look at $P go!
[09:44] **The Moleman** : b GDX puts Dec 16 20 strike
[09:44] **Cowboy** : FCX sl hit 13.65 out C's +0.05
[09:44] **The Moleman** : nice tradin $P
[09:44] **MoneyPenny** : thank you Pinky!
[09:44] **Cameron O** : sold some of my GDX calls from straddle back
[09:44] **Lesley C** : /GC bouncing off level called a few minutes ago, weak bounce.
Next old print 1244.00
[09:45] **Lesley C** : then 1240.20
[09:46] **Stefanie K** : wow, those 22 puts are 300% ROI

You can see we were mostly trading stocks and options on **GDX**, **DUST**, and **JDST**. This was one of the best trading days the Java Pit has ever had. Many of my traders were making 1000 percent or more return on investment on their **GDX** puts.

The biggest question I get asked is how long are these prints good for? Are they just good for one day, one week, or longer? My answer is always the same. They are good for as long as the Dark Pool is still trading off of them. These computers are still buying and selling at these specific levels. Follow the smart money.

That's exactly what happened with **IAU**. It continued to move down until it hit that magic buying level of $10.85 from February 2, 2016.

Ten months later, the Dark Pool was still buying at $10.85. Look at this next daily chart where **IAU** bounced right off that level:

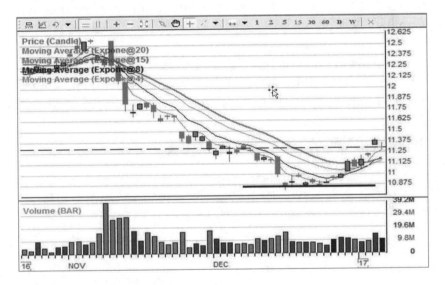

Even though we did not get any big prints there this time, it still bounced right on that magical level in December. I have drawn a line of the Dark Pool level on the chart.

Swing Trading Seasonal Patterns

In this book I've covered many examples to illustrate how powerful prints are. However, these print levels are even more powerful when you combine them with seasonality. Seasonality is identifying periods of strength or weakness over specific timeframes. My favorite website that I use for this is www.equityclock.com.

Seasonality alone isn't good enough for me. I need to see the Dark Pool buying along with seasonality to find the highest probability swing trades. Just for the record, I consider swing trading as holding a stock overnight. It doesn't matter if you are holding it for one night or a year.

I'm going to walk through one of my "hottest" seasonal swing trades of 2017. The trade happened last summer on Procter and Gamble (**PG**).

In the chart below, you'll see a 20-year seasonal chart for **PG**. You can see that it usually bottoms out in June before making a huge run up all the way to December.

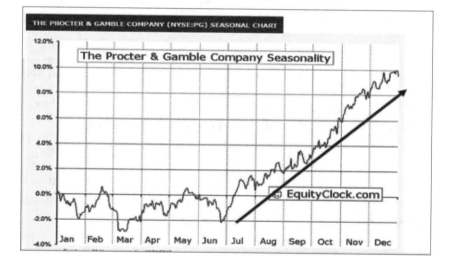

Below is a daily chart of **PG** for May of 2017. You can see the major trend lines that I drew above the price to show resistance around $90. At the time, **PG** was trading at $87 and so there was adequate room for a nice trade up to $90. If **PG** broke above $90, there is room to $92.

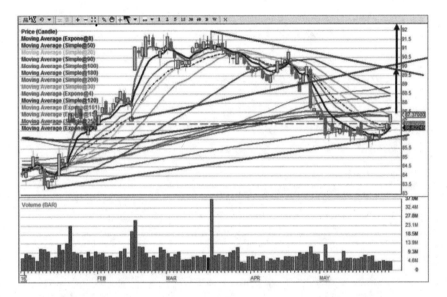

We needed one more thing for us to make this trade. We needed to see some big prints, and we did in the beginning of May. The big guys came in and started buying **PG** at $86.50. We had two huge trades on May 2 of 1.3 mil shares and 740K sharse, both at $86.50. Below you'll see the picture of their trades from LIVEVOL® Pro:

Time	Symbol	Qty	Price	Exchange	Condition	Market
12:08:41	PG	1335197	86.5000	NQNX	Regular	86.49 x 86.5
12:29:23	PG	740339	86.5000	NQNX	IntermarketSweep	86.48 x 86.49
16:00:36	PG	729531	86.2200	NYSE	Closing	86.21 x 86.22
16:00:36	PG	729531	86.2200	NYSE	MarketOnClose	86.21 x 86.22

If **PG** stayed above $86.50, it was going to be a hot trade, and it did! By mid-June the price hit the $90 target. It then pulled back in July before running up again, peaking at $94.67 on September 20.

> As a brand new trader, I joined the The Java Pit after watching Stefanie's Counting the Cards series. I have been listening to the whispers every day and practicing paper trading around the prints. So far, many of the setups have developed on my trades based on the whispers. I can hardly wait to learn how to use the prints with options.
>
> I have looked at several trading rooms but really enjoy the variety of traders in the Java Pit and respect the conservative approach that Stefanie takes towards the market. As a new trader, I'm looking for strategies and education that will offer me longevity.
>
> Sheri Hadfield

Chapter *9*

HOW TO SPOT A CORRECTION BEFORE IT HAPPENS

Not too many people are going to tell you that the market is rigged. Ladies and gentlemen, I want you to be the judge. I, Stefanie Kammerman, will provide the evidence: evidence of manipulating trades being executed in the darkest Dark Pools. I will shed light on some of these illicit trades in these next two chapters. Keep in mind, there are so many more examples I want to show you, but I would have to write a whole other book. Perhaps I'll put them into my next book.

The "Sharks in the Dark Pool" are trading way ahead of corrections, insider trading, and, in some cases, even terrorist attacks. I will show you many of these trades and teach you how to spot them so that in the future you will be able to profit off this manipulation.

How many of you would like to see what a correction looks like before it happens? Whenever I present this question at one of my presentations, I have everyone's undivided attention and all eyes are glued to my screen. This is one of my favorite moments as a teacher. I love to shed light on manipulation and help traders save their hard-earned money. By calling for a correction in November 2015, I saved one of my students, Neil Hadden, over $100K. Neil met me at the TradersEXPO in 2014. Being a diamond member gave him privileges to sit in on all the master classes. He told me that my class was one of the best he had ever seen. He had no clue about the Dark Pool and he was so excited to learn more.

Over the past five years, I've gained thousands of followers by calling the last 10 corrections on social media before the correction happened. It's always good to see what numerous corrections look like because the money flow does change. Sometimes the money goes into the bonds and the dollar, while other times it flows into gold. Every workshop that I have put out to date has at least one correction in it. Some even have more than one. I show you the Dark Pool prints, and where the money is flowing.

Workshop	Date of Correction
Counting the Cards of Wall Street Part 1	Aug 5, 2013
Counting the Cards of Wall Street Part 2	Jan 17, 2014
Counting the Cards of Wall Street Part 3	Jul 7, Sep 9, 2014
Finding the T-spot	Nov 28, 2014
What's inside the Candle	Feb 26, 2015
How to Profit off the Dark Pool	Nov 4, 2015
Prints and Patterns	May 20, Jul 20, 2016
Trading Options with the Sharks in the Dark Pool	Three corrections: Jul 20, 2015; Jun 10, 2016; Sep 8, 2016

Calling corrections has its perks. After I saved Neil over $100K, he and his wife Jodi take me out for dinner at every show they attend to say thank you. The correction I am going to share with you in this book is one of the most talked about ones: the big flash crash of summer of 2015.

Most traders believe that the correction came out of nowhere. My trading room knew that the Dark Pool was selling heavily at the end of July and again on August 20.

On July 20, 2015, we spotted a massive three million print before the bell even rang on the **SPY** at $212.72. Here is my tweet at 9:14am ET from that day.

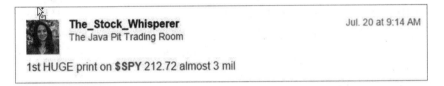

The_Stock_Whisperer   Jul. 20 at 9:14 AM
The Java Pit Trading Room

1st HUGE print on $SPY 212.72 almost 3 mil

We do not normally see such a large trade on the **SPY** before the market opens. It woke us up to pay more attention to the next set of prints. Here are all the trades greater than 500K that day for the **SPY**. You can see we didn't get too many.

Individual option trades

Select   SPY(W) Jul24'15 175 P (0)   ▼
or
Input   SPY SPY(W) Jul24'15 175 P 07/20/2015

Underlying trades

Time ▲	Symbol	Qty	Price
09:13:25	SPY	2957000	212.7200
14:04:09	SPY	1900000	212.8225
14:23:59	SPY	501233	212.5285

The Dark Pool has a special signature share size. The share size usually starts with either a 501K, 502K, or 503K. We call them the Levi's. It's a running joke we have in our trading room, a reference to Levi's 501 jeans. We know it's the big guys like Goldman Sachs who are trading it. Coincidentally, Goldman built Levi Stadium in Santa Clara, California.

I don't call a correction after we see just one of these 501K Levi prints like we had on July 20. I need to see a lot more. I also need to see the big guys selling across the board. I need to see late sell prints as well on the Russell 2000 ETF (**IWM**), or the Nasdaq ETF (**QQQ**), along with some prints on fear like the iPath S&P 500 VIX Short-Term Futures ETN (**VXX**). I also need to see big prints on bonds or gold. Money flow needs to shift out of the markets into safety.

The **SPY** was hitting a major resistance on the daily chart. Look at this next chart:

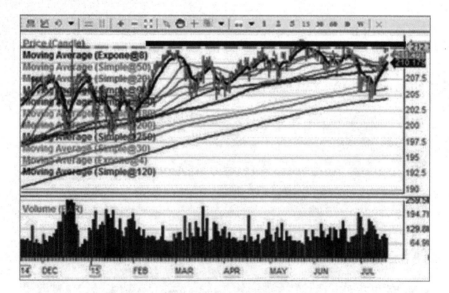

Guess what we spotted the next day? We spotted some fear kick in. The big hedge funds will put on protection rather than sell their portfolio when a correction is coming. They put on protection by buying the **VXX**. It just so happened we spotted a huge million share print on the **VXX** at $16.35. We don't see that every day, so I felt the need to tweet it out. I tweeted "**VXX**, one million shares...just saying..." This means that you need to pay attention!

Here is a picture of the trade. It was the only large trade that day on fear. It was enough to grab my attention.

Time ▲	Symbol	Qty	Price
13:09:45	VXX	1000000	16.3500

Select VXX(W) Jul24'15 10 P (0)
or Input VXX VXX(W) Jul24'15 10 P 07/21/2015
Underlying trades

We had two smaller trades the next day on the **VXX** adding up to 500K.

Time ▲	Symbol	Qty	Price
13:14:34	VXX	300000	16.2750
14:34:14	VXX	200000	16.1500

Select VXX(W) Jul24'15 10 P (0)
or Input VXX VXX(W) Jul24'15 10 P 07/22/2015
Underlying trades

This was enough to pop the **VXX** up to over $18 the next two days. Fear was on the rise and so were bonds. We spotted money moving into the Bond ETFs. This was the safety play.

We spotted a 581K share print on the iShares 20+ Year Treasury Bond ETF (**TLT**). Here is my tweet on it:

> **The_Stock_Whisperer**   Jul. 21 at 1:12 PM
> The Java Pit Trading Room
>
> **$TLT** 581K $118.82....bonds anyone?

The next day we spotted an even bigger print on **TLT**. This one was for 800K at $119.68.

Select	TLT(W) Aug07'15 103.5 P (0)		
or Input	TLT TLT(W) Aug07'15 103.5 P 07/22/2015		

Underlying trades

Time ▲	Symbol	Qty	Price
15:14:31	TLT	800000	119.6800

After these buy prints came in, **TLT** made a huge move, rallying from $118.82 up to $128.

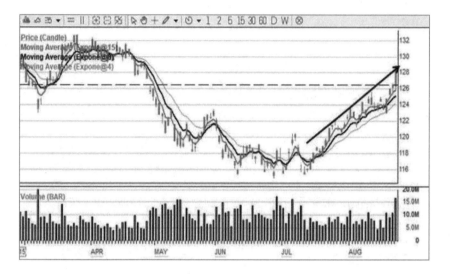

Even though we can see that the money flow was going into the bonds, we still need to see the big boys selling in the Dark Pool before we call a correction. That's exactly what we started to see.

On July 22, at 10:31am ET, I spotted quite a few late Dark Pool 501K Levi prints on the SPY at $211.82. I turned bearish at this point. This was the last piece of evidence I needed for confirmation. I immediately tweeted this out, letting all my followers know that the Dark Pool was selling.

The_Stock_Whisperer   Jul. 22 at 10:31 AM
The Java Pit Trading Room

FRESH off the Printing press **$SPY** late dark pool sell prints $211.82 bearish below
Bearish

These prints were late sell prints. The **SPY** was at $211.52 when these were printed, already 30 cents below the Dark Pool prints.

Here is a picture of the **SPY** five-minute chart along with my block trade indicator. The line on the chart shows the $211.82 Dark Pool level. The **SPY** was trading lower. Smart money was selling. You can also see the 501K prints to the left of that.

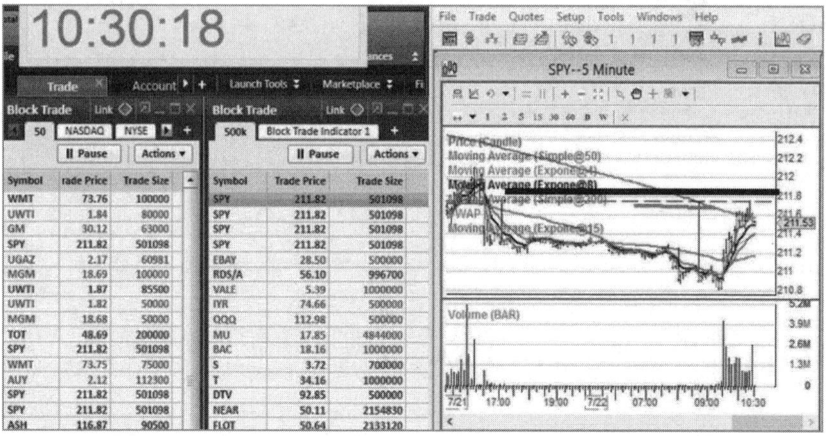

Here is the Level 2. The bid at the time this print came in was at $211.52 and the offer was at $211.53.

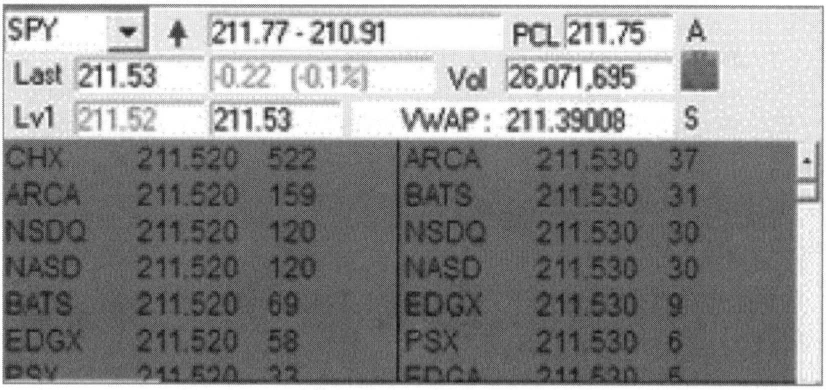

We had nine of these late Dark Pool sell prints that day.

Select or Input	SPY(W) Jul24'15 175 P (0) ▼
	SPY SPY(W) Jul24'15 175 P 07/22/2015

⦿ Underlying trades

Time ▲	Symbol	Qty	Price
10:29:16	SPY	501098	211.8164
10:29:16	SPY	501098	211.8164
10:29:47	SPY	501098	211.8164
10:30:14	SPY	501098	211.8164
10:37:28	SPY	501098	211.8164
10:38:30	SPY	501098	211.8164
15:03:01	SPY	501098	211.8164
15:26:35	SPY	1002196	211.8164
16:00:00	SPY	1006117	211.3700
16:00:00	SPY	1006117	211.3700
16:01:16	SPY	501098	211.8164
16:01:45	SPY	501098	211.8164

7/22/2015	
Hi: 211.77	
Lo: 210.89	
O : 210.91	
C : 211.37	
V : 88,667,920	
210.154	
AVG:210.262	
AVG:211.039	
AVG:211.644	

We turn bearish if we close below this $211.82 level, which we did. Here is the Open, High, Low, Close (OHLC) for that day. You can see the **SPY** closed 45 cents below the Dark Pool level. The more telling thing, however, is that the Dark Pool price is above the high of the day. Notice that the high of the day was $211.77. The Dark Pool level is five cents above that, at $211.82. This means that the **SPY** did not even print at the Dark Pool level that day, but that these were prints from the prior day being reported late. I had always been taught that all the exchanges were required to report their trades within three hours of execution. These prints seem illegal.

This was just the beginning of the heavy selling to come. We have seen this pattern so many times before. The next day, July 23, we spotted a lot more late Dark Pool sell prints on the **SPY**. Here is my tweet from that day.

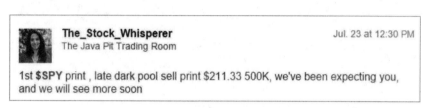

The_Stock_Whisperer   Jul. 23 at 12:30 PM
The Java Pit Trading Room

1st $SPY print , late dark pool sell print $211.33 500K, we've been expecting you, and we will see more soon

Late Dark Pool prints are like cockroaches. When you see one, there are always more waiting in the wings, ready to come out. The **SPY** was trading down at $210.20 when this trade appeared. Here is the five-minute chart on the **SPY**. Again, I have drawn a line at the Dark Pool print level. You can see this was clearly reported late.

You can see on the Level 2, the bid was $210.20, and the offer was $210.21 at the time that this late Dark Pool sell print came in at $211.33.

That's over an hour and a dollar late! At the same time that we were seeing these late Dark Pool sell prints on the **SPY**, we were also receiving late Dark Pool sell prints on the Russell 2000 index ETF (**IWM**). The Russell 2000 index (**RUT**) is an index measuring the performance of 2,000 small-cap companies. It serves as a benchmark for small-cap stocks in the United States.

After spotting millions of these late Dark Pool sell prints coming across the tape on **IWM** at $124.88, I had to tweet it out A.S.A.P. Here is my tweet:

The_Stock_Whisperer   Jul. 23 at 1:24 PM
The Java Pit Trading Room

Millions of late dark pool sell prints across the tape on $IWM @ 124.88 Uh huh, we saw this coming $$

Here is a five-min chart on the **IWM** from that day. I have drawn a line on the print level.

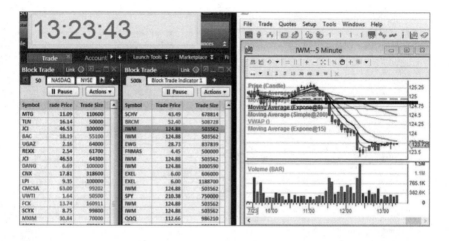

You can see the **IWM** was trading much lower when these prints appeared. The big boys sold at the top and were now reporting these trades to us, again, over an hour late, and over a dollar late.

The bid on **IWM** was $123.72 and the offer was at $123.73.

Here is a picture of all those 503K trades on July 23, on the **IWM** along with the OHLC.

Time ▲	Symbol	Qty	Price
12:15:21	IWM	503562	124.8823
12:39:12	IWM	503562	124.8823
12:40:00	IWM	503562	124.8823
12:44:04	IWM	503562	124.8823
12:46:56	IWM	1000590	124.8824
12:51:54	IWM	503562	124.8823
13:02:39	IWM	503562	124.8823
13:04:19	IWM	503562	124.8823
15:11:08	IWM	503562	124.8823
15:15:28	IWM	503562	124.8823
15:17:25	IWM	503562	124.8823
15:48:51	IWM	503562	124.8823
15:56:59	IWM	503562	124.8823
16:40:37	IWM	1005209	124.8823

7/23/2015	
Hi:	125.39
Lo:	123.3
O :	125
C :	123.57
V :	39,712,139
118.873	
AVG:124.919	
AVG:124.736	
AVG:124.442	

Eight million late Dark Pool sell prints printed on July 23 at $124.88. The closing price of the **IWM** was $123.57, $1.31 below the Dark Pool prints. This was another bearish signal.

The next day we spotted some more late Dark Pool sell prints on the **IWM**. I just could not help myself. I tweeted some more about it:

> **The_Stock_Whisperer**   Jul. 24 at 1:17 PM
> The Java Pit Trading Room
>
> FINALLY, here comes the late dark pool sell prints, those sneaky armani suits $IWM $SPY `Bearish`

The **IWM** was trading down over a dollar when these prints came in. This, in conjunction with the late **SPY** sell prints, was telling. Sometimes, the market will immediately drop after we see this type of pattern. This time, the market didn't immediately drop. The market churned sideways over the next week or so, giving investors and traders plenty of time to get out of long positions and put on some protection. You could also go short and profit when you see this happening. I was warning all my traders in the room that a big correction was coming. Most of my traders listened to me and saved themselves a lot of money. Many of them went short and made a lot of money following the Dark Pool prints.

On August 11, 2015, I warned all my followers on social media by putting out this next tweet. *"Be careful out there, we're headed for a correction here, put protection on, more sell prints coming in"*

> **The_Stock_Whisperer**   Aug. 11 at 11:04 AM
> The Java Pit Trading Room
>
> Be careful out there, we're headed for a correction here, put protection on, more sell prints coming in

It was not just one sell print. It was a succession of sell prints across the board on the **SPY**, the **IWM**, and the **QQQ**. It was seeing the prints on fear coming in on the **VXX**, and the money flowing into bonds that led me to call another correction.

I couldn't believe that we were about to get another correction and I was going to miss it. I was scheduled to go on my first vacation in five years. I hate missing even one day of the market. I was scheduled to go on a cruise to Alaska. No internet for an entire week. I just knew this was when the market was going to crash.

I needed some peace of mind. After seeing these sell prints coming in, I knew a correction was imminent; however, I didn't know the exact date it would happen. Options are a great way to put on some protection just in case something happens while you are away. I would have jumped overboard on this cruise ship if it happened and I didn't put on any protection. I decided to put on a Hail Mary Trade. A Hail Mary trade is one in which I go fairly deep out of the money (OTM). The idea of this type of trading is that a large move is anticipated, and because we had all the setup for a correction, this made sense for me. I would never go so far OTM any other time.

On August 13, 2015, I bought the $200 strike way out of the money Sept 11 expiration puts on the **SPY** for $0.85. The **SPY** was trading at $209 when I put this trade on, so these puts were $9 OTM. I only bought two contracts. Yes, I am still kicking myself under the table. This trade cost only $179 to place. Here is a snapshot of the entry.

| 08/13/15 | 3298 | Option | Buy Open | 2 | SPY Sep 11 '15 $200 Put | Mkt | Day | Mkt | 0.85 | Executed |

Whenever I go small, big things happen. The week I was on that cruise with no internet, the **SPY** crashed from $209 down to $197. I returned on Monday, August 24, to watch the **SPY** drop even more. It fell from $197 to a low of $182.40. Here is a snapshot of my exit. I sold my puts on August 24 for $15.79, making over 1650 percent ROI!

| 08/24/15 | 3301 | Option | Sell Close | 2 | SPY Sep 11 '15 $200 Put | Mkt | Day | Mkt | 15.79 | Executed |

I exited my trade when the **SPY** bounced up and broke above $185. I didn't peg the bottom, but I did okay. This trade paid for my cruise to Alaska.

Here is the whole trade.

SPY Sep 11 '15 $200 Put	2	08/13/2015	0.85	179.6	S	08/24/2015	15.79	3,148.39	2,969	Short	Edit

I risked $179 on this trade and my reward was $2,969.

I would never have put on this Hail Mary trade if we didn't see
those late Dark Pool sell prints. I didn't even show you the **QQQ**
prints that came in while I was on my cruise. These trades should
be illegal. That's how deceptive they are, but there are loopholes.
Remember those **SPY** prints on July 22 that printed five cents
above the high of the day? The trades you are about to see are not
three hours late. They are 24 hours late. I always thought that if
you did a trade today, you had to report that trade today. What I
started to notice was that there were quite a few very late prints.
These prints clearly were not executed today because the price
never traded at that level. The price suggests that they had been
traded the day before.

That's when I learned of a very special Dark Pool Secret. I was
on the way to a dinner with some traders and folks from the
Bank of Montreal. This floor trader spilled the beans. I asked
him how it was legal that I was seeing these very late trades. He
told me of a very special loophole. If Goldman Sachs crosses
a trade from their desk in New York across the ocean to their
desk in London, they have 24 hours to report this trade.

That made a lot of sense to me. How else are they going to sell
millions of shares without moving the market down?

This is precisely what they did on the **QQQ** while I was on my cruise. Even though I was not there to call it out in my trading room, I had taught all my traders what to look for. This is what I want to teach you.

Check out these very late Dark Pool prints. These are 24 hours late on the **QQQ**.

Time ▲	Symbol	Qty	Price
10:39:30	QQQ	410687	110.1122
10:56:27	QQQ	410687	110.1122
10:57:03	QQQ	410687	110.1122
11:01:25	QQQ	410687	110.1122
11:19:48	QQQ	410687	110.1122
11:37:30	QQQ	410687	110.1122
12:19:02	QQQ	410687	110.1122
12:22:36	QQQ	821373	110.1122
12:54:26	QQQ	410687	110.1122
12:54:55	QQQ	410687	110.1122
14:11:32	QQQ	264000	107.6727
15:49:10	QQQ	501064	110.1122
16:00:00	QQQ	647339	107.0800
16:00:00	QQQ	647339	107.0800
16:12:46	QQQ	501064	110.1122
16:41:59	QQQ	500360	110.1122
16:44:09	QQQ	500320	110.1122
16:51:27	QQQ	501044	110.1122

Select QQQ Aug21'15 70 P (0)
or Input QQQ QQQ Aug21'15 70 P 08/20/2015
Underlying trades

8/20/2015	
Hi:	109.46
Lo:	107.07
O :	109.11
C :	107.08
V :	57,747,349
104.612	
AVG:110.371	
AVG:109.904	
AVG:109.178	

The Dark Pool signature share size on the **QQQ** is different than the **IWM** and the SPY. We have observed that the Dark Pool prefers to do 410K and 411K share lots. There are a few 501Ks too. You can see the high of the day is $109.46. The Dark Pool prints were all executed at $110.11. The Dark Pool sold and hid these trades from us. When we see this, we know it's time to sell. There are always a lot more where these came from.

In every correction that I have spotted, I have seen this maneuver. The Dark Pool was also selling heavily on the **SPY** on August 20. Millions of late Dark Pool sell prints came across the tape all day long at $208.28, even though the **SPY** was dropping.

Time ▲	Symbol	Qty	Price
10:07:10	SPY	500927	208.2862
10:30:28	SPY	500924	208.2862
12:59:02	SPY	500924	208.2862
12:59:29	SPY	500924	208.2862
13:00:05	SPY	500924	208.2862
13:01:37	SPY	500924	208.2862
14:19:19	SPY	500919	208.2862
14:19:52	SPY	1001849	208.2862
14:24:42	SPY	500924	208.2862
14:29:25	SPY	1001849	208.2862
14:43:15	SPY	500924	208.2862
15:42:12	SPY	500874	208.2862
15:42:12	SPY	500874	208.2862
15:47:59	SPY	500874	208.2862
15:52:05	SPY	500874	208.2862
16:01:28	SPY	500874	208.2862
16:04:21	SPY	500874	208.2862
16:05:02	SPY	500874	208.2862
16:11:52	SPY	500924	208.2862
16:12:41	SPY	500874	208.2862
16:17:51	SPY	500924	208.2862
16:29:09	SPY	500874	208.2862

Select or Input: SPY Aug21'15 120 P (0) / SPY SPY Aug21'15 120 P 08/20/2015 — Underlying trades

```
8/20/2015
Hi: 208.2865
Lo: 203.9
O : 206.54
C : 203.97
V : 194,327,884
199.403
AVG:208.718
AVG:208.128
AVG:207.117
```

You can see in this OHLC and the prints on the LIVEVOL® Pro software that even though the **SPY** closed at $203.97, these late $208.28 prints kept coming. Note that these prints all happened at the $208.28 high of the day. This was smart money selling at the top.

Wait, we're not done yet. I must show you the trades on the **IWM** that day. These trades were clearly executed on August 19 but not reported until August 20. Seven and a half million shares were printed at $119.50. The high of the day on August 20 was only $118.61.

Select or Input	IWM Aug21'15 60 P (0) ▼
	IWM IWM Aug21'15 60 P 08/20/2015

○ Underlying trades

Time ▲	Symbol	Qty	Price
09:53:05	IWM	503289	119.5022
10:17:58	IWM	503289	119.5022
10:26:03	IWM	503289	119.5022
10:27:23	IWM	1006679	119.5022
11:02:56	IWM	503340	119.5022
11:03:44	IWM	503340	119.5022
13:29:00	IWM	503340	119.5022
13:30:34	IWM	503340	119.5022
13:41:29	IWM	503289	119.5022
15:20:07	IWM	503289	119.5022
15:26:25	IWM	503289	119.5022
15:54:03	IWM	503303	119.5022
15:57:44	IWM	503289	119.5022
16:00:00	IWM	2192858	116.3900
16:00:00	IWM	2192858	116.3900
16:15:04	IWM	503289	119.5022

8/20/2015
Hi: 118.61
Lo: 116.39
O : 118.41
C : 116.39
V : 51,879,763
113.885
AVG:120.445
AVG:119.568
AVG:118.676

These trades had the same Dark Pool signature. They were all 503K lots. They were all executed at the same price of $119.50. As you can see, it wasn't just one day of massive selling. The Dark Pool unloaded millions of shares at the top.

Time ▲	Symbol	Qty	Price
10:38:17	QQQ	500000	105.3531
12:42:11	QQQ	630000	104.6500
13:28:17	QQQ	410736	107.0474
13:34:59	QQQ	410736	107.0474
13:37:07	QQQ	410736	107.0474
13:39:32	QQQ	410736	107.0474
13:42:26	QQQ	410736	107.0474
14:20:23	QQQ	410736	107.0474
15:24:03	QQQ	410695	107.0474
15:28:18	QQQ	410695	107.0474
15:36:07	QQQ	821391	107.0474
15:44:35	QQQ	821391	107.0474
15:59:38	QQQ	410695	107.0474
16:00:00	QQQ	899154	102.4000
16:00:00	QQQ	899154	102.4000
16:07:21	QQQ	492870	107.0473
16:15:57	QQQ	410695	107.0474
16:31:22	QQQ	1500870	107.0474
17:08:35	QQQ	1002848	107.0474
18:07:01	QQQ	1262500	102.4000

Select or Input: QQQ Aug21'15 70 P (0)
QQQ QQQ Aug21'15 70 P 08/21/2015
Underlying trades

```
8/21/2015
Hi:  106.47
Lo:  102.4
O :  105.57
C :  102.4
V :  97,763,445
101.474
AVG:109.375
AVG:108.236
AVG:106.467
```

The next day, on August 21, the Dark Pool was reporting the sales of millions of shares of the **QQQ** at $107.04, where the high of the day was only $106.47.

The biggest day of all was on August 24. This is what we call seller's exhaustion. I had to take three separate pictures of all the prints from August 24 to capture them. At least 15 million printed at $102.47. **That's over $1.5 Billion dollars!**

Time ▲	Symbol	Qty	Price
Select or Input	QQQ(W) Aug28'15 85 P (0)		
	QQQ QQQ(W) Aug28'15 85 P 08/24/2015		
● Underlying trades			
09:30:00	QQQ	793951	94.1700
09:30:00	QQQ	793951	94.1700
09:43:18	QQQ	410555	102.4766
09:43:49	QQQ	410555	102.4766
09:45:06	QQQ	410555	102.4766
10:00:18	QQQ	410555	102.4766
10:04:40	QQQ	410555	102.4766
10:07:02	QQQ	410555	102.4766
10:07:44	QQQ	410555	102.4766
10:07:44	QQQ	410555	102.4766
10:08:16	QQQ	410555	102.4766
10:10:25	QQQ	821110	102.4766
10:19:02	QQQ	410555	102.4766
10:19:40	QQQ	410555	102.4766
10:20:08	QQQ	410514	102.4766
10:22:39	QQQ	410555	102.4766
10:23:14	QQQ	410555	102.4766
10:30:07	QQQ	410555	102.4766
10:30:34	QQQ	410514	102.4766
10:30:58	QQQ	400000	100.2000

| Select | QQQ(W) Aug28'15 85 P (0) ▾ |
| or Input | QQQ QQQ(W) Aug28'15 85 P 08/24/2015 |

● Underlying trades

Time ▲	Symbol	Qty	Price
10:39:59	QQQ	410555	102.4766
10:43:57	QQQ	410555	102.4766
10:44:44	QQQ	410555	102.4766
11:38:32	QQQ	410514	102.4766
11:47:44	QQQ	410555	102.4766
11:48:10	QQQ	410514	102.4766
12:11:40	QQQ	410555	102.4766
12:12:57	QQQ	821110	102.4766
12:30:56	QQQ	410555	102.4766
12:33:23	QQQ	410555	102.4766
12:39:22	QQQ	865001	102.2775
12:44:40	QQQ	410555	102.4766
12:46:38	QQQ	384682	102.0000
12:48:47	QQQ	410555	102.4766
12:52:20	QQQ	410555	102.4766
12:52:54	QQQ	410555	102.4766
13:06:55	QQQ	410555	102.4766
13:12:21	QQQ	410555	102.4766
14:02:08	QQQ	410555	102.4766
14:25:58	QQQ	410555	102.4766

Select

or

Input

QQQ(W) Aug28'15 85 P (0)

QQQ QQQ(W) Aug28'15 85 P 08/24/2015

● Underlying trades

Time ▲	Symbol	Qty	Price
12:48:47	QQQ	410555	102.4766
12:52:20	QQQ	410555	102.4766
12:52:54	QQQ	410555	102.4766
13:06:55	QQQ	410555	102.4766
13:12:21	QQQ	410555	102.4766
14:02:08	QQQ	410555	102.4766
14:25:58	QQQ	410555	102.4766
15:10:55	QQQ	410514	102.4766
15:23:15	QQQ	410514	102.4766
15:31:41	QQQ	410514	102.4766
15:50:56	QQQ	410555	102.4766
16:00:12	QQQ	410514	102.4766
16:05:41	QQQ	410514	102.4766
16:16:59	QQQ	441000	99.5500
16:41:40	QQQ	1000000	98.6125
16:41:40	QQQ	500000	98.6125
17:04:31	QQQ	501000	102.4766
17:05:51	QQQ	501000	102.4766
17:14:34	QQQ	1001754	102.4766
17:37:40	QQQ	3000358	102.4766

On this daily chart of the **QQQ**, you can see the high volume on August 24, dropping it down to $84.74 before bouncing up.

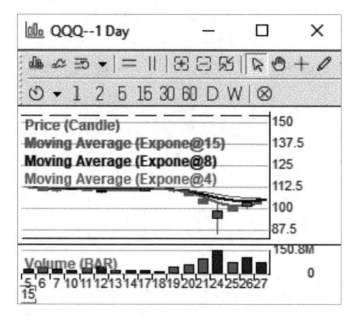

8/24/2015
Hi: 102.53
Lo: 84.74
O : 94.23
C : 98.46
V : 150,829,863
90.8843
AVG:108.011
AVG:106.064
AVG:103.264

You can see these prints just keep going and going. Sellers exhaustion happens when most traders in the same asset are short, leaving a few investors to take the other side of the transaction. Exhaustion signals the reversal of the current trend because it illustrates excess levels of supply or demand.

Guess what happened next? The Dark Pool started buying the **QQQ**. Look at these next trades on August 26. Millions of shares were executed at $98.07.

Time ▲	Symbol	Qty	Price
10:47:19	QQQ	410485	98.0759
11:20:50	QQQ	410444	98.0759
12:03:15	QQQ	700000	99.7700
13:29:29	QQQ	594000	100.2000
13:52:10	QQQ	410485	98.0759
14:25:55	QQQ	1000000	100.3050
14:31:10	QQQ	410485	98.0759
14:53:53	QQQ	410485	98.0759
15:07:37	QQQ	410485	98.0759
15:39:05	QQQ	410485	98.0759
15:44:52	QQQ	410485	98.0759
15:44:52	QQQ	410485	98.0759
15:48:41	QQQ	410485	98.0759
15:53:59	QQQ	410526	98.0759
16:02:30	QQQ	410526	98.0759
17:22:04	QQQ	500260	98.0742

Select or Input: QQQ(W) Aug 28'15 50 P (0)
QQQ QQQ(W) Aug28'15 50 P 08/26/2015
Underlying trades

8/26/2015	
Hi: 103.23	
Lo: 98.93	
O : 100.96	
C : 103.03	
V : 104,103,817	
96.5383	
AVG:106.303	
AVG:104.011	
AVG:101.929	

How do you know a correction is over? When we get late Dark Pool buy prints. On August 26, 2015, **QQQ** never traded at $98.07. The low of the day was $98.93.

QQQ ended up closing way above these late Dark Pool buy prints at $103.03. Around six million shares printed at that $98.07 level. Keep in mind, this is the same pattern on every correction.

Just in case you were wondering, the **SPY** also had late Dark Pool buy prints on August 26. Millions of prints came in all day long at $187.19, but the low of the day was $188.37.

Time ▲	Symbol	Qty	Price
10:03:11	SPY	1001527	187.1929
10:16:21	SPY	500764	187.1929
10:16:21	SPY	500764	187.1929
10:32:50	SPY	500713	187.1929
10:32:50	SPY	500713	187.1929
10:52:03	SPY	500713	187.1929
10:52:03	SPY	500713	187.1929
11:00:04	SPY	500746	187.1929
11:00:39	SPY	500713	187.1929
11:10:17	SPY	500713	187.1929
11:17:58	SPY	1001427	187.1929
11:19:32	SPY	500713	187.1929
11:28:19	SPY	500746	187.1929
11:28:24	SPY	500746	187.1929
11:31:10	SPY	500713	187.1929
11:33:59	SPY	1001327	187.1929
11:37:40	SPY	500746	187.1929
11:49:14	SPY	1001327	187.1929
12:11:44	SPY	500663	187.1929
12:11:44	SPY	500663	187.1929
12:20:04	SPY	1001327	187.1929
12:22:33	SPY	500663	187.1929

Select or Input: SPY(W) Aug28'15 100 P (0) / SPY SPY(W) Aug28'15 100 P 08/26/2015 — Underlying trades

8/26/2015	
Hi: 194.79	
Lo: 188.37	
O: 192.06	
C: 194.46	
V: 339,256,986	
188.179	
AVG:201.827	
AVG:197.890	
AVG:193.942	

These late Dark Pool buy prints kept printing all day long. If you want to get out your calculator, you can, but I'm going to estimate it around 23 million. Smart money is buying the bottom here.

| Select | SPY(W) Aug28'15 100 P (0) ▼ |
| or Input | SPY SPY(W) Aug28'15 100 P 08/26/2015 |

⦿ Underlying trades

Time ▲	Symbol	Qty	Price
12:24:19	SPY	500663	187.1929
12:27:58	SPY	500663	187.1929
12:30:12	SPY	500746	187.1929
12:35:29	SPY	1001327	187.1929
12:42:28	SPY	500746	187.1929
12:42:36	SPY	500746	187.1929
13:11:56	SPY	500663	187.1929
13:12:43	SPY	500663	187.1929
13:13:37	SPY	500663	187.1929
13:13:37	SPY	500663	187.1929
13:15:39	SPY	500663	187.1929
13:56:41	SPY	500713	187.1929
13:56:41	SPY	500713	187.1929
14:13:31	SPY	500663	187.1929
14:31:30	SPY	750995	187.1929
14:31:59	SPY	500663	187.1929
14:31:59	SPY	500663	187.1929
15:12:03	SPY	500713	187.1929
15:53:49	SPY	500764	187.1929
15:59:49	SPY	500814	187.1929

We did not get any massive Dark Pool buying on the **IWM**, but we got enough on the **SPY** and the **QQQ** to know this was the bottom. Here is the daily chart of the **SPY**:

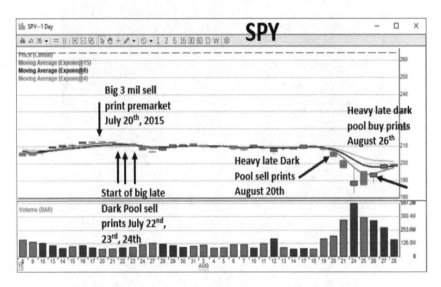

You can see where the Dark Pool started selling and where they started buying. We had plenty of time to prepare for this flash crash.

Dear Stefanie,

Thank you for helping me with the timing ideas I needed to exit my former employer's 401(k) plan and go to cash prior to rolling over to a self-directed IRA and the new employer's 401(k).

Here's what happened.

My former employer sold the division of the company for which I worked. As part of this transition, I needed to sell the investments in my old 401(k) and go to cash before I could re-deploy funds to the new 401(k) plan, and to new self-directed IRAs. The main problem I faced was that the 401(k) was doing so well primarily in an Emerging Markets Fund, and S&P Index Fund at Merrill Lynch, that I was reluctant to "pull the plug."

As a member of The Java Pit at The Stock Whisperer since June of 2017, I decided I would simply "follow the prints," as you suggest: Bullish above, Bearish below. By waiting for massive prints we saw in the Java Pit in the SPY (15 Million+); EFA (84 Million); and IEFA (65 Million) on the 29th and 30th of January 2018, and the bearish market action which followed, I made the decision to "Go To Cash," by selling everything on January 31st.

The next few days were shocking. Had I stayed in my investments, I would have lost over $11,000 on February 2nd, and over $43,000 by February 9th. Because of The

Stock Whisperer, I was able to re-invest my $482,996.

The next few days were shocking. Had I stayed in my investments, I would have lost over $11,000 on February 2nd, and over $43,000 by February 9th. Because of The Stock Whisperer, I was able to re-invest my $482,996 retirement fund at 7-10% below the highs of late January. I didn't buy back at the exact lows; in fact, I'm still re-deploying these funds with a variety of managers, including my new 401(k) plan, but all at serious discounts to the market highs of late January 2018. By the way, I've heard some pretty interesting comments from professional traders when I tell them I went to cash on January 31st. They probably don't believe me until they get my statements, and even then they think it was just blind luck. I don't care what they think. I saved a bundle of hard-earned cash.

Every day in the Java Pit, you teach us to be patient, wait for the prints, and make sure we're "Bullish above, Bearish below." Since last June, not counting the 401(k) experience recounted above, I've added to my personal trading account (which started at just $20,000) by following you in The Dark Pool, while also working my full-time job. We've made big tradeson quite a few stocks and to be honest, we've had some losers, too. It helps during our live sessions with you every day to hear directly from you when you're getting out of a trade that didn't work, and to benefit from your calm demeanor when we're killing it in the trades that do work out just exactly as you called them. I've become a much less emotional, more disciplined trader since joining The Java

Pit. It's also fair to say that I'm having a whole lot more fun. You give your traders the quiet confidence that we have powerful information which is likely to move the market, then when we see the move begin, we simply get on board and catch the wave (follow the prints).

Stevan R Davis
"Mr. Sinatra"

Chapter 10

THE DARKEST POOLS
(WHAT NOBODY ELSE WILL TELL YOU)

I have never worked for any of these large, full-service investment banking firms like Fidelity, Charles Schwab, or Merrill Lynch. I've never worked for any brokerage firms. To be quite honest, they would never hire me. I am a whistleblower. I had an interview a few years ago where I boasted about all the corrections I have called before they happened. I thought they would want somebody to help save their clients' money by being able to call a correction. Let's just say my phone never rang. These big brokerage firms do not want you to take money out of your accounts when a correction is coming. They are nervous you will never put it back.

Working for myself gives me the ability to call it like it is. I don't have to worry about answering to any institution. When I see manipulation occurring, which for me is almost daily, I can call it out. It's great to be able to do this without worrying that I may be fired the next day.

What you are about to see in this chapter are the Darkest Pools. These are trades that most people, especially investment advisors, would be afraid to show you. These trades are the very trades that I feel compelled to show you. I feel everybody is entitled to see what really goes on in the Dark Pools. I know that this is my calling. This is what I was born to do.

Over the past 25 years, I have witnessed so many kinds of trades. Just when I thought I had seen them all, I would see something that I could not explain. It was so odd. It was so peculiar and unexpected.

On March 21, 2016, I spotted gigantic prints on **TVIX**. For those of you who have never heard of **TVIX**, here is a quick definition. According to its prospectus, the value of **TVIX** is closely tied to twice the daily return of the S&P VIX Short-Term-Futures.

While **TVIX** trades like a stock, it is not a stock. It's an ETN, an exchange traded note. ETNs are unsecured, unsubordinated debt obligations of the company that issues them. They have no principal protection. They are not insured or guaranteed by the FDIC. Although an ETN's performance is contractually tied to the market index that it is designed to track, an ETN does not hold any assets.

Most ETNs are decaying instruments, and **TVIX** is no exception. It is constantly rolling down the hill. The best way I describe what this means to my students is to correlate it to buying a brand new car at the dealership. The salesman convinces you that this lime green Mercedes is the hot new car this season. You pay full price for this high demand car and you happily drive it home. Your spouse takes one look at it and tells you that they would be never be caught dead in that lime green car. They do not care how hot it is right now.

To save your marriage, you drive it back to the dealer the next morning. When you ask the dealer to trade it in for a white

Mercedes at the same price, the dealer tells you, "Oh no, we can't do that. We will take it back, but we will have to give you $5,000 less than what you paid for it. That car is not brand new anymore. You put some miles on it."

This, ladies and gentlemen, is like **TVIX**. It is that lime green Mercedes that you want to return the next morning. It is going to decay overnight, and you will get less money for it the next day. The only way you will get more is if something horrific happens to spike volatility up.

The average daily volume is 21 million shares on **TVIX**. There are no options available. There are no shares of a corporation, no sales, quarterly reports, or profit and loss statements. It does not have a P/E ratio and no, there is no prospect of getting dividends.

It's very similar to the **VXX** in that it measures fear. When traders are fearful that the market is going to have a correction, we will start to see large trades on the **VXX**, **TVIX,** and sometimes **UVXY**, which is the ProShares 3x VIX Short-Term Futures ETF. I showed you in the last chapter how we got that big one million print on the **VXX** when we were about to have a correction. That is normal trading behavior. We expect to see that in the tape.

What I witnessed on March 21, 2016 was very different.

We were not having a correction. There were no late Dark Pool sell prints on the **SPY**, the **IWM**, or the **QQQ**. The market was very quiet as these massive prints started to come across my tape.

At 10:26am ET, I spotted the first large print on **TVIX**. Six million printed at 5.08. This was a late Dark Pool buy print.

Here is my first tweet that day on it:

> **The_Stock_Whisperer**
> The Java Pit Trading Room
>
> Mar. 21 at 10:26 AM
>
> Very late HUGE dark pool buy print **$TVIX** 6 mil@5.08 WOW!!!!!!!

The reason these were late buy prints was that **TVIX** was already trading up at $5.36 when these printed.

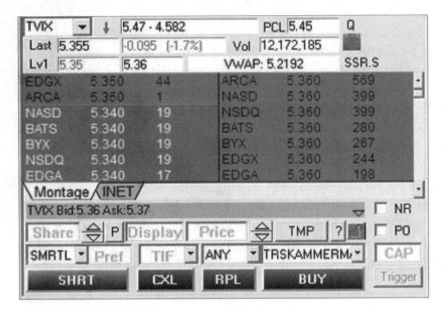

The bid was $5.35, and the offer was $5.36 at the time that this six million share trade printed at $5.08. You can see in my tweet that I posted quite a few exclamations points.

Here is a picture of the print in my block trade window along with the five-minute chart:

Do you see that crazy wick down on this chart? It looks like **TVIX** dropped down from $5.25 down to $4.58. Those trades are what we call fat finger trades. The trade was canceled.

Let me show you those cancellations:

10:06:13	TVIX	3000	4.5820	NYSETRF	Canceled/IntermarketSweep
10:06:13	TVIX	500	4.5820	NQNX	Canceled/IntermarketSweep
10:06:13	TVIX	300	4.5820	NQNX	Canceled/IntermarketSweep

As if six million wasn't a big enough trade to alarm us that something was going on, we spotted another massive trade one hour later.

At 11:35am, I tweeted once again. I spotted a five million print on **TVIX** at $5.06.

The_Stock_Whisperer　　　　　　　　　　Mar. 21 at 11:35 AM
The Java Pit Trading Room

Another HUGE late dark pool **$TVIX** 5 milllion shares from yesterday 5.06 Never seen this before on **$TVIX**

In my tweet I let everybody know that I have never seen this before on **TVIX**.

The volume on **TVIX** was already up to 21 million shares, and it was only 11:35am. The Bid was $5.25, and the offer was at $5.26. This was another late Dark Pool buy print.

Wait folks, don't go anywhere. We got another biggie coming. This was the biggest one of all.

<u>Ten million printed on **TVIX** at 12:29pm at $5.06.</u>

This was a monster print. Of course, I had to tweet once again. I never would have noticed these prints if I did not have a block trade indicator with Dark Pool data feed scanning the entire market all day long.

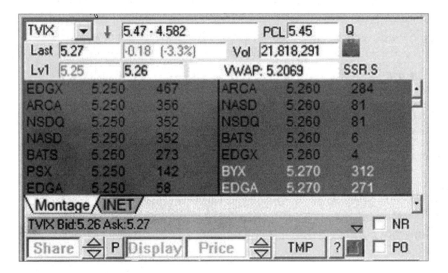

Here is my last tweet that day on **TVIX**:

The_Stock_Whisperer
The Java Pit Trading Room

Mar. 21 at 12:29 PM

Another HUGE monster late print $TVIX WOW!! 10 million $5.06

I still had no clue what was going on. My trading room put on protection just in case something horrific was going to happen. Even though we had a heads up that something was brewing, we were not prepared mentally for this next event. This was an event that would change hundreds, if not thousands of lives.

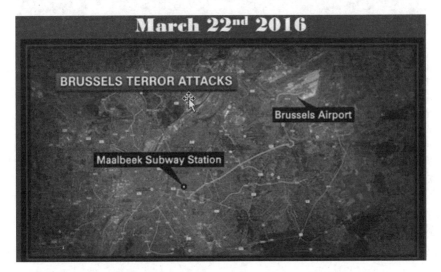

The next morning, March 22, 2016, three coordinated nail bombings occurred in Belgium. Two were at the Brussels Airport, and one was at Maalbeek metro station in Brussels. In these attacks, 32 victims and three suicide bombers were killed. Over 300 more people were injured. Another bomb was found during a search of the airport. Islamic State of Iraq and the Levant claimed responsibility for the attacks. The bombings were the deadliest act of terrorism in Belgium's history.

I was speechless, and for me that is rare. Could it be that somebody knew this attack was going to happen and they were trying to profit off it?

I did a little more research and found that there were very heavy prints on **TVIX** also on March 17 and 18.

On those two days, 15 million more printed from $5.01 to $5.57. Most of the volume occurred on the lower end closer to $5. Prior to March 17, there was nothing big printing on **TVIX**.

The **TVIX** went from no interest at all to high volume interest days before this attack.

What do you think **TVIX** did after this attack? You guessed right. It went up as high at $5.68 before dropping back down again. Remember, this is a lime green Mercedes that is constantly depreciating over time.

Here is a picture of the daily chart so you can see the pop and drop:

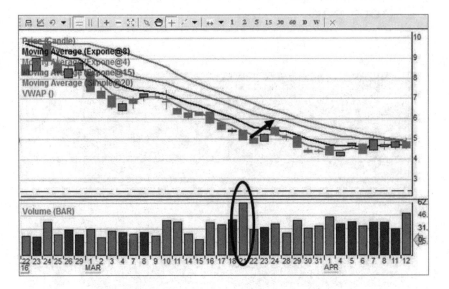

I have circled March 21, 2016, the day before the attack where we got the highest volume of prints.

Did the trader that bought **TVIX** sell it and take their profit? There were no big sell prints on **TVIX** the next day or any day after. Perhaps they were expecting a larger move off that heinous act of terror? Or possibly they were planning another attack. Well, that is exactly what happened.

Pakistan explosion leaves many dead at Lahore park

🕐 17 minutes ago | Asia

March 27th 2016

AFP

The blast happened in the early evening

On March 27, 2016, an explosion in the Pakistani city of Lahore killed 74 people and injured 362 more. The blast was in a large park in the southwest of the city. The explosion happened at the main gate to the park. A splinter group of the Pakistani Taliban, Jamaat-ul-Ahrar, claimed responsibility for the attack.

Massive prints followed by two massive terrorist attacks. Coincidence or insider trading? You be the judge. I'm just providing the evidence of the trades. You can make up your own mind.

Insider Trading

Insider trading occurs in many ways. You may know somebody that knows something and tells you something that you should not know. I do not get tips. I do not get phone calls. I do not pay for special research either. I do not need any of that. I just follow the guys that do.

On September 6, 2016, at 3pm, I spotted a gigantic print on Wells Fargo (**WFC**). The print was for 2.6 million at $49.84. This was extremely unusual. In fact, I do not ever remember such a large print on **WFC**.

Let me show a picture of that trade:

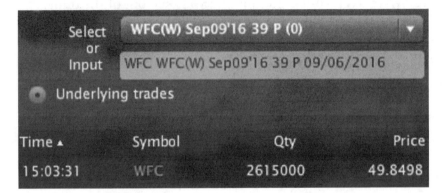

This print was so unusual I had to put **WFC** in my Whisper of the Day video the very next morning on September 7. Here is the link in case you want to listen to it: https://www.youtube.com/watch?v=5KqrdYeQfqE

> **#whisperoftheday9-7-16**
> The Stock Whisperer @ The Java Pit • 430 views • 1 year ago
>
> The Stock Whisperer's Morning Whisper is: $SPY $GDX $WFC $JPM $MT $AKS $USDU #morningwhisper #hotstockoftheday #todayswhisper #whisperoftheday. For more please

Here is what I posted up in the announcement tab that morning:

> **08:37 Stefanie Kammerman** : Today's whisper GDX bullish above 28.50: AKS bullish above 4.62 (prints there yesterday) : WFC bearish below 49.75, bullish above 50 (prints at 49.84 yesterday) MT bullish above 5.25 (prints) : USDU bullish above 26, bearish below 25.90 (prints 25.97 yesterday)
> **08:38 Stefanie Kammerman** : also JPM bullish above 67.50 bearish below 67 prints at 67.26 yesterday

My trade setup on **WFC** was bearish below $49.75 and bullish above $50. If smart money was buying **WFC** at $49.84, it should have easily broken above $50. If smart money was selling **WFC**, it should easily break down below $49.75. I like to keep it simple. You always want to stay on the right side of the prints. Never hold onto your trade if you are on the wrong side. ALWAYS keep your emotions and your ego out of the trade. Trading should purely be mathematical.

As soon as the bell rang, **WFC** dropped below the print. Likewise, JPMorgan Chase & Co (**JPM**) dropped below the $67.26 print I posted in the announcements. I do not trade the first 10 minutes because as you know, that is the shake out period.

At 9:31am, I posted up in our trading room that these banks were trading lower.

> 09:31 **Stefanie Kammerman**: WFC dropping
> 09:31 **Stefanie Kammerman**: jPM below the prints

At around 10:40am , we had a bit of a rally and **WFC** came up to test the $50 level; however, it was unable to break through. Here is my post regarding that in the room:

> 10:40 **Stefanie Kammerman**: WFC unable to break above 50

At 10:47 am, I announced that it was time to buy puts on **WFC**. It had moved below my Whisper level $49.75. I had turned bearish on it. It could not break above $50. When stocks test resistance and move lower below the prints, that is a very bearish sign.

> 10:47 **Stefanie Kammerman**: B puts on WFC

Guess what happened two days later? News broke out on **WFC**. Not good news. Let's just say I wasn't surprised.

Wells Fargo fined $185M for fake accounts; 5,300 were fired

Kevin McCoy , **USA TODAY**   *7:47 a.m. EDT September 9, 2016*

On September 9, 2016, Wells Fargo was fined $185 Million for fake accounts. Wells Fargo employees created unauthorized bank accounts to boost sales, prompting the bank to fire 5,300 employees.

At 11:09am, Dick Bove warned investors on CNBC that Wells Fargo has displayed "beyond outrageous behavior" and investors should sell the stock.

I wonder who was selling their stock two days earlier? **WFC** ended up getting crushed. In this chart, you can see what happened in light of the prints as well as the news.

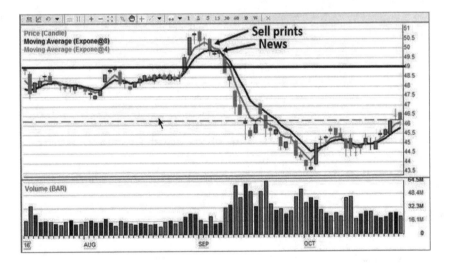

It fell right through $49 support all the way down to $43.50.

This Whisper caught the attention of Will Deener, a special contributor for The Dallas Morning News. He wrote an article featuring this manipulation on "How everyday investors can make money by peeking into the Dark Pools."

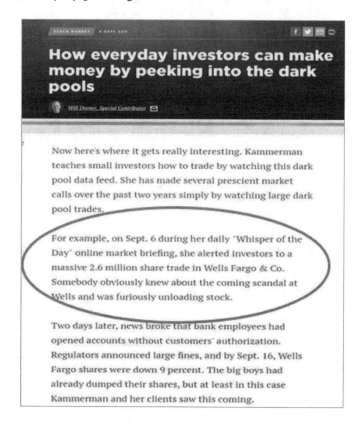

It was so great to be able to help many of my traders by seeing these Dark Pool prints before the news came out.

Secret Signal Trades

There have been a few times throughout the years where we have seen prints that were far away from where an index was trading. We call these Dark Pool Secret Signal Trades. These are a much rarer type of Dark Pool trade.

The Dark Pool will signal to us where they are possibly going to take that stock or ETF.

On November 28, 2017, I tweeted that I had spotted one of these special Secret Signal Trades on the **QQQ**.

At 9:08am, we saw a 2.3 million print on **QQQ**. What was so special about this print was the price. It printed at $153.81. This wasn't a late buy print. The **QQQ** was trading at $156.34 at the time this printed. The day before, **QQQ** traded between $155.83 and $156.56. In other words, the price of this print was nowhere near where recent trades had taken place on **QQQ**.

Below is my tweet:

The_Stock_Whisperer Nov. 28 at 1:46 PM
We had an unusual print this morning on $QQQ , it appeared nowhere else but my Schwab software

09:08:43

Symbol	Trade Price	Trade Size		Symbol	Trade Price	Trade Size		Symbol	Trade Price	Trade Size
MTU	6.91	125000		QQQ	153.81	2300000		QQQ	153.81	2300000
STM	24.22	60000		CHU	14.60	451954		FB	183.03	186160
QQQ	153.81	2300000		AAGIY	34.00	504387		AAPL	174.09	405663
INVH	23.39	115400		VMBS	52.67	1207453				
SQ	40.20	99100		T	34.68	482219				
RDS/A	64.16	125000		MSFT	83.87	604913				
FRCOY	37.17	234109		AAPL	174.09	405663				
FRCOY	37.17	234109		IQV	102.25	500000				
MARA	5.04	100000								
NVDA	215.25	223218								

I want to blow up that picture so you can see it better.

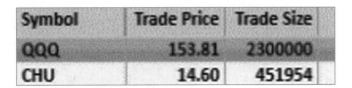

Symbol	Trade Price	Trade Size
QQQ	153.81	2300000
CHU	14.60	451954

11/27/2017	11/28/2017
Hi: 156.56	Hi: 156.69
Lo: 155.83	Lo: 155.7
O : 156.2	O : 156.52
C : 156.19	C : 156.59
V : 22,653,389	V : 25,227,320
154.82	156.137
AVG:153.539	AVG:153.830
AVG:154.181	AVG:154.482
AVG:155.123	AVG:155.449
AVG:155.768	AVG:156.097

Here are the two OHLCs from November 27 and November 28, 2017. You can see that the **QQQ** did not trade anywhere near $153.81. Normally I would have been baffled by this, but I have seen this before. I spotted it on the IWM and the SPY in the past. This was the first time I had ever seen it on the **QQQ**.

Here is the chart of the **QQQ** showing you that it hadn't traded at $153.81 for five days. This was a secret Dark Pool signal of where they were going to take the **QQQ**.

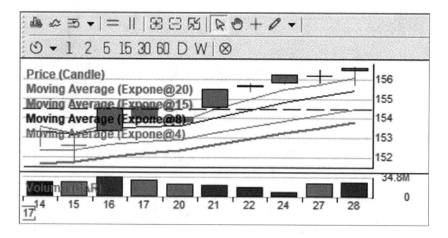

Each time we have seen this in the past, the stock or ETF ended up going to that price shortly thereafter.

Here is the weird part. Where is this volume? At the time the **QQQ** printed 2.3 million shares, there was only 112K of volume that morning.

This next picture is the Level 2 and time and sales. You can see at 9:13am ET, there was still only 112K volume traded. Also, this print didn't show up anywhere else. No other platform showed this print.

Only Charles Schwab had this trade. This has been the case quite a few times in the past as well.

My traders in my room were all over it. Wall Street Wiz was the first to call it out.

> 09:07 **Wall_St_Wiz .** : QQQ 2.3 million 153.81 huge

I immediately posted it in the announcement tab in my trading room.

> 09:11 **Stefanie Kammerman** : Here is a very bizarre Dark Pool print 2.3 mil just printed on $QQQ $153.81 This is very rare bit we\'ve seen it before

John looked it up on his Lightspeed™ platform and realized the trade didn't exist there.

> 09:08 **JohnEm .** : that QQQ not on Lightspeed

I shared with the room during my morning meeting of the possibility of the **QQQ** coming down to the price of the print. I posted it up again in our trading room.

> 09:59 **Stefanie Kammerman** : Be very interesting if QQQ comes down to 153.81

That afternoon, I posted up in the room that I was taking a very low risk "lottery ticket trade". I was buying very inexpensive far out of the money puts on **QQQ** for 25 cents.

Steve, a new trader in the room had never seen this before and thought it was an error. I reassured him it was not. We had seen this before. This is the Darkest Pools.

> 13:48 **Stefanie Kammerman** : B QQQ puts lotto ticket based on that print this morning. very small risk trade .25
> 13:48 **Steve** : Stef, that print had to be an error, don't you think?
> 13:48 **Stefanie Kammerman** : No Steve
> 13:48 **Stefanie Kammerman** : I don't think
> 13:48 **Stefanie Kammerman** : I have seen it a few times before

Here is a picture of all the prints from November 28, 2017. You can see there was no 2.3 million print listed on this LIVEVOL® Pro software. In fact, there was very little volume that day. We knew that something wasn't right.

Time ▲	Symbol	Qty	Price
10:07:35	QQQ	799900	156.2774
12:43:39	QQQ	411343	156.1984
14:31:54	QQQ	1003710	156.1984
14:36:28	QQQ	411343	156.1984
14:36:47	QQQ	411343	156.1984
15:52:09	QQQ	411343	156.1984

Guess what happened to **QQQ** the next day? It came down and hit that Secret Dark Pool print level. Let me show you the daily chart on the **QQQ**:

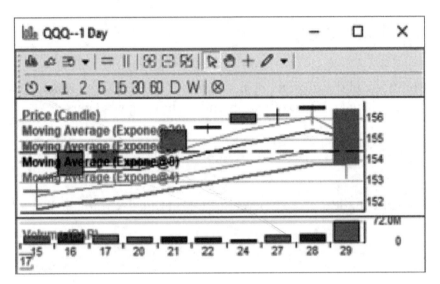

Here is the OHLC for November 29. The **QQQ** came down to $153.12 and closed at $153.86, just five cents shy of that secret print!

11/29/2017
Hi: 156.45
Lo: 153.12
O : 156.45
C : 153.86
V : 71,986,338
154.844
AVG:153.832
AVG:154.404
AVG:155.096
AVG:155.202

Below are the posts from our live trading room that day:

Wall Street Wiz and Ron both announced that **QQQ** was dropping down.

09:32 **Wall_St_Wiz** . : QQQs weak
09:32 **Ron** : QQQ dropping

Many of my traders were also buying the puts on **QQQ** off the secret print. James, aka Rockstar, bought the December Wk1 155.50 strike puts.

> 09:46 **Rockstar . :** b QQQ 155.5P 12/1

Ron noticed the divergence between the **QQQ** and the other indices. The **QQQ** was the only index showing weakness.

> 09:47 **Ron :** this is quite the divergence QQQ and other indicies Tech under fire

Rockstar made a nice 20 percent ROI on this day trade.

> 09:56 **Rockstar . :** s QQQ p +20%

I was holding onto mine for that $153.81 target. Rustygoose also thought it was headed there as well.

> 10:02 **Rustygoose . :** Looks like the QQQ are headed for that odd print

I called out lower lows for the **QQQ** while SuzieQ was calling out big prints on the **XLF**, the financial ETF. All day long my traders call out highly unusual prints.

> 10:16 **Stefanie Kammerman :** QQQ's new new
> 10:16 **Stefanie Kammerman :** low
> 10:16 **SuzieQ :** XLF 27.34 2m
> 10:16 **Stefanie Kammerman :** dumping

I started to scale out of my **QQQ** lotto puts. It's always a great idea to take money off the table when you hit 100 percent ROI. That's doubling your money.

Our traders are very supportive of each other. We all work together all day long in the pit. Wall Street Wiz called out that **QQQ** was going for that crazy print.

10:24	**Wall_St_Wiz .** :	QQQs nLOD at s5 pivot
10:25	**Wall_St_Wiz .** :	buckle up more down
10:25	**David** :	QQQ testing 20dma
10:25	**Verminator .** :	44.49-44.62 INTC closed 44.73
10:25	**Wall_St_Wiz .** :	QQQ going for that crazy print yesterday
10:25	**Stefanie Kammerman** :	crazier things have happened

I scaled out of another fourth of my puts, making 120 percent ROI.

10:37 **Stefanie Kammerman** : out of another 1/4 QQQ crazy puts .68 120% ROi

I scaled out of another fourth, making 300 percent ROI. We were so close to the crazy secret print. This is when you want to take your profit.

11:02 **Stefanie Kammerman** : out of another 1/4 QQQ .93 WOW over 300%

Christopher, a new member in my room, had an amazing trade on his puts. He made well over a $1.00 on them.

11:03 **Cristopher** : QQQ s 1/2 +1.00

12:04 **Cristopher** : out last QQQ b Puts at .33 sold for 1.90

Gerald also did well on his puts, profiting 43 cents.

12:23 **Gerald** : AAPL, p + .32; SPY, p + .21; QQQ, p + .43

As you can see from the three examples I have shown you in this chapter, there are many ways the market is manipulated. I've also shown you how being able to spot these manipulations can help you profit from them. I have so many more examples from over the years that I just didn't have time to show you here.

I'm confident the information and examples in my book can make you a better trader, regardless of your style of trading. However, for most people there is a gap between understanding the Dark Pools and knowing how to use the prints to profit.

As you've read, you've probably had a lot of questions about some of the principles, what type of trade you might use in each circumstance, or how you would execute given your situation. It's impossible for me to anticipate and answer all the questions in a single book, or to give you all the ways you can trade using what I've taught you about the Dark Pools.

But, don't worry! I have a solution. I have lots of additional help available for those of you who are serious about improving your results in the market – regardless of your experience level.

There is so much more to learn and so much opportunity to profit. You've seen example after example of chats and calls from my trading room. I've spent decades teaching others how to do what I do and I've loved every minute of it! In fact, you might say I'm a little bit addicted to it. I love seeing the light go on for traders (new or seasoned) and then to hear the stories of how their results have changed dramatically. It's one of the few things in life that feels as good to me as executing a killer trade.

If an opportunity to work with me and my team sounds good to you, you're in luck. We'd like to spend even more time showing you how to use the Dark Pools to trade stocks, options or pretty much anything else you'd like to trade. I've made it my mission to shed a light on the Dark Pools, how they can manipulate the markets and most importantly, how YOU can profit from them and protect yourself from market corrections. I know this information can make a difference for you, so I'm offering everyone who gets my book a free consultation with a member of my team.

Pretty cool, huh?

We'll discuss your experience level, where you're starting from, what you want to accomplish, the type of trading you'd like to do, your risk tolerance, etc. Then, based on that, we'll suggest additional training you may need to increase the odds you'll hit your trading goals.

No two traders are alike and not everyone needs to start in the same place or go down the same road. That's why we start with a consultation. It might be that you only have a few questions you need answered, and with those answers and this book you're good to go. It could be that you need additional help, but we won't know until we talk.

Call **1-800-544-6044** or go to
www.DarkPoolConsultation.com right now
and get your **FREE one-on-one
consultation** scheduled.

By the end of your consultation, you'll have a clear understanding of how we can help you improve your trading results and what it will take for you to reach your goals.

Here's what you can expect:
- Interact with me and my team as you take advantage of Dark Pool trades
- Master the fundamentals that every trader needs to know
- Track Dark Pool trades from home

- Attend live, interactive classes that deliver practical help and demonstrations
- Discover the trading style that best fits your financial goals
- Learn advanced strategies from our collection of knowledge and experience in different specialties

By combining the Dark Pools with our training, we'll take out the guess work and show you how you can profit in any market condition.

Many traders learn the hard way, through expensive trial and error. This is a cost-effective way for you to master the craft of trading. No one cares about your money more than you. We'll teach you how to grow it and protect it.

Go to **www.DarkPoolConsultation.com** or call **1-800-544-6044** to schedule your FREE consultation.

Go to **www.DarkPoolConsultation.com**
or call **1-800-544-6044**
to schedule your **FREE consultation**.

This one call could completely change the way you trade and set you on the path to achieving your financial goals. Contact my team now, while you're thinking about it. Don't put it off!

We'll decide together whether or not working with my team is the right thing for you.

If nothing else, remember this... **Bullish above, bearish below, no thinking!**

Stefanie Kammerman

I attended Stefanie's recent Workshop on How to Profit Off the Dark Pool and it was amazing. She pulls back the curtain and reveals the monster Dark Pool prints big Wall Street trading firms try to hide...and shows you how you can spot them yourself and profit from them. The Big Boys can run, but they can't hide from Stefanie! I highly recommend you check out The Stock Whisperer and discover one of the most fascinating ways to trade that you've ever seen.

Nick Moccia
Publisher, Weiss Education

Appendix
MEET THE PITTERS

Our traders in the Java Pit come from all over the world. They are very special characters. Years ago, I told them I would make them famous. This is their moment. Many of these traders came to me with little or no knowledge of trading, while others have added incredible knowledge to our room. It's a very open community. My traders have the floor to share whatever tools or strategies have worked for them. We all share the same passion. We have the same dream. What we have learned is that we can really grow if we work together as a team.

Let me introduce you to the "Pitters"

Wayne, aka the Cowboy, is from Texas. You probably would have guessed that even if I hadn't told you. He was our Trader of the Year in 2014. He is one of our oldest members. He paper traded the longest before taking the real money plunge. I have total respect for that. I will never forget the morning he came into the Java Pit all upset with me. I thought I had done something wrong. After hours of suspense, he finally told me his problem. He had to pay taxes that year because of me. He made too much money. Oh boy did we laugh after that. He has contributed in so many ways to the Pit over the years. We have learned so much from him, especially from his j-hook presentations. We just wish we could learn where we can get one of his Dumbo scanners that seems to call things right on. We love you Cowboy!

> *Stefanie is as passionate about her trading as she is about teaching. She gets excited when new traders join the room and everyone in the room welcomes you as a friend. She goes out of her way to get you up to speed and helps you learn so that you do not lose money. No upsales or gimmicks, just good education. Her method is remarkably consistent.*
>
> *The Cowboy*

Vernon, aka The Verminator, is from New Jersey. He is a huge fan of our T-Spot t-shirts. He adds so much quality to our trading room by posting up Excel spreadsheets of all the Dark Pool prints every day. He was our Trader of the Year for 2017. We had such a blast having dinner with him at Carmine's Italian Restaurant after the New York TradersEXPO. He's one of those special people that make you smile every day.

> *I just love everything about this room and its people! It's the perfect trading environment with the best technicals and numerous, very savvy helpers.*
>
> *Vernon P*

Celeste, aka Money Penny, aka Celessio, aka Martini girl, aka The Crypto Queen, is from Mississauga, Ontario. Celeste has had the most nicknames in Java Pit history. I would pay to see her do stand-up comedy. She is that funny. I have enjoyed so many dinners with her after the Toronto MoneyShow. Not a day goes by when she doesn't ask me what I think about gold. She says, "If Stefanie could teach me how to trade, she can teach anybody." She tried to escape boot camp after the first day, but stuck around and worked her butt off. I have only had to erase a few of her comments over the years due to the graphical nature. She keeps us laughing all day long while we trade. She clearly has worked the hardest to overcome her obstacles in life.

> *So if you're like me, and I'll bet a lot of you are, I'm sick and tired of these "fake" testimonials from "real" people. I have tried enough scams... oops I mean trading rooms and various courses to know the poop from the real deal. This IS the REAL DEAL! I could never, with a clear conscience, write a testimonial for a load of rubbish! I don't even know where to begin to explain how the Stock Whisperer has changed my life. The learning never stops in the Java Pit!*

Not only does Stefanie teach us invaluable skills, and you will be amazed how much you don't actually know. The Dark Pool in itself is worth it! Besides Stefanie's coaching, the amount of brain power in the Java Pit will blow your mind! Other more advanced and experienced traders call out information all day long and are eager to help you. There is NO PUMPING in this room. If you actually want to start making money from your trading, join us. Stefanie and Matt, this is also a heartfelt thank you to both of you for all you have done and do for us on a daily basis. You have turned my trading around 180 degrees.

Celeste xo

Robert B, aka Rockstar Trader, is from Toronto. He loves our Dark Pool Stock Whisperer chocolate bars and does a great job helping us out at the Toronto MoneyShow and the New York TradersEXPO.

Thank you, Robert, for all your support over the years.

Stefanie, Matt and the Pitters. If you're lost they will be your guide. In the first five minutes of talking to Stefanie I knew this trader knew what she was talking about. When she mentioned "Dark Pool" and where she worked, she had me. Those first five minutes were the most valuable minutes of my life as a trader. The wealth of knowledge being in

The Java Pit is unmeasurable. They have become family. A very positive atmosphere.

Something Jaythetrader said to me during my recent trip to the NYC Traders Expo made me realize why we're all there. To learn and to pass on our knowledge to others and Stefanie does this so well...thanks Coach, Matt and the Pitters.

Robert Badke aka RockstarTrader

Amit, aka Bam Bam, aka Crypto King, is from Frisco, Texas. He trades Bitcoin all night long, which is why he is usually the first trader in the room at 6am. Amit excels in Elliott wave analysis and loves to warn us before the big moves come.

I just wanted to let you know that you guys do a really good job. I'm glad I decided to join the Java Pit. The room is full of experienced traders and newcomers from different markets and different parts of world, sharing ideas, learning from Stefanie. " Sharing is caring" is motto of room and Stefanie is very successful in embedding that into the room. My accuracy improved after joining the Java Pit. Here dark pool print strategy is so simple yet so powerful . Thanks, guys!

Amit

Ron, aka Wall St Wiz, is from British Columbia. We don't think he's human. He earned his nickname by being our Trader of the Year for 2016. His charts are out of this world! You will want to frame them and put them on your wall as stock art. He consistently calls out his trades all day long with target exit levels. One thing we learned about Ron is that he is usually early, so make sure you set your watch 30 minutes slower than his. He leans to the bear side and always puts NSFW (not safe for work) on each of his trades. This means do not follow him in his trades unless you know what you are doing.

> *Stef's illuminated insight of levels and Dark Pool action is an added asset to any trader using indexes, futures, options and stocks. a definite addition to your bottom line.*
>
> *Wall St Wiz*

Bob E, aka Hot Dog, is from Montana. You guessed it. He loves to eat hot dogs, drink beer, and ride horses. We were so happy to meet him at the Vegas show where he shared his favorite trade with us that day. The $2 Nathan's Famous hot dogs down the block. They were selling the $10 hot dogs at Caesars Palace, so thank you Bob for always sharing those great trades with us. He is a great asset to our Pit.

My name is Bob. I have had a short career as a trader. I am approaching retirement age and am entering a different relationship with the stock market and investing. I have had a trading and training relationship with Stefanie for about two years and want to say a couple of things about my experience. First, I would say that Stefanie is the real deal. She delivers everything that she promises up front. The most valuable things I have learned from Stef are how to identify and follow the Dark Pool and find the levels for entry and exits. I've made hundreds of trades based upon those levels. Stef has also been prompt in responding to questions and problems and in a courteous and professional manner, another characteristic that makes her the "real deal"...

Bob E

Ricki, aka The Options Whisperer, from Colorado, came to me years ago. She needed my help. She was trained as an engineer and had to change her career. She told me that she knew how to trade options but needed help trading stocks. I promised her that if I taught her how to trade stocks, she needed to teach me how to trade options. Ricki was my absolute best student. She worked the hardest and memorized all my rules. There are days I feel I have cloned myself when I hear Ricki doing a meeting in our trading room. She now teaches our traders in the Java Pit how to trade options around the Dark Pool, as well as how to take advantage of earnings volatility using options. She also helped me edit this book you are reading. We all thank you for that and everything you have taught us in the Pit. We have inspired each other for years and years. Ricki is one of my angels down here on earth.

> "Stefanie has totally transformed me as a trader. We trade off the Dark Pool prints ... watching to see where the smart money is buying or selling, and coat-tail off their trades. No trading system is perfect, and I have some small losing trades, but when these trades work, as they often do, I'm often able to make double and triple digit ROIs on my trades. I can't trust anyone who says they have no losing trades. Stefanie doesn't sugar-coat trading as something that anyone can make millions overnight. She's real, and she's realistic. She teaches us to expect losing trades, but shows us how we can keep those losses small, at the same time teaching us how to make much larger winning trades. In the Java Pit, her live trading room, she is forever teaching and helping traders to manage their risks and make some great trades. Under Stefanie's guidance, we support each other, we learn from each other, we make money together, and we have a lot of fun. I can't imagine trading without Stefanie."
>
> *Ricki*

 **Suzanne, aka Suzie Q**, is from Edmonton, Alberta. She is one of the fastest to call out all the unusual prints in the Pit. Some days we have a contest to see if we can beat her. She has worked so hard over the years, and it is paying off for her. We all love what she adds to our room, and I look forward to meeting her in person one day soon.

My Java Pit name is SUZIEQ. I have been with Stefanie Kammerman and a member of the Java Pit for 1 year and 9 months. I first heard of Stefanie at an investment seminar in Edmonton, Alberta. I was there to learn how to develop a low risk portfolio. Stefanie's presentation impressed me. However, it took a long time for me to join her Java Pit because I did not want to trade. I wanted a low risk portfolio. As an investor, I was told trading was risky so I thought Stefanie's room was not for me. At that time, I did not know that what she was talking about could lower the risk of investing.

Eventually, I realized I needed The Stock Whisperer and the Java Pit. I was missing a very important aspect of owning a stock. What were the large fund managers doing? Are they selling or buying? I could see these large trades on my platform and realized an ETF or stock would move up or down significantly after these trades were made. Sometimes it would happen right away, other times it took time, even weeks. It became clear that knowing about these trades helped determine when to purchase a stock/ETF or reduce/sell off a position. I was always told to follow the money, but it was a struggle to do that. I was using a free service that followed money flow and watched for block trades. But it wasn't very productive or efficient. Thankfully, I remembered Stefanie talking about the Dark Pools and block trades. I signed up to the Java Pit room and also took the first boot camp I could. Thank you.

Susanne P

Lionel L, aka the Golden Boy, is from Hamilton, Ontario. We go way back, trading together for almost a decade. Our favorites have been GLUU, CAT, and you guessed it, GOLD! I haven't met Lionel in person yet, but when you have spent eight hours a day with somebody in a trading room for almost ten years, you feel like you already know them quite well. It's been my pleasure getting to know you Lionel, and I hope to get to meet you in person soon.

Doug, aka FX Power Lines, from Vancouver, took my T-Spot to the next level. He is a special effects manager for some major television shows, including the X-Files and Once Upon a Time. His charts have the most special effects, and we are blessed to have him post them up in our room. We have met several times over the years and have shared some very funny moments, especially the time we snuck him into tea at the Gatsby Mansion Inn in Victoria.

Lesley, aka the Golden Glider Girl, from British Columbia, brought volume spread analysis (VSA) into our trading room. I love when I can learn something new from traders that come into our room. It does not matter how long you have been trading, there is always something new you can learn. Thank you, Lesley, for sharing.

❝I have been a Java Pit member for about 5 years. I can't imagine trading without access to the large prints - that would be like trading blind. Stefanie's analysis and rules are valuable for both new and seasoned traders.❞

Lesley

Angela, aka the Futures Teller, was a commodities broker on the floor of the Chicago Board of Trade (and later the CME Group after the merger). She's a crazy futures trader who stays up all night to trade. We love when she shares her stories of the bears that come to visit her house. Angela's success has been a huge inspiration for me as a female and as a trader. She is such a special woman. We are so honored to have her in our room. She gives and shares her knowledge without any expectations in return. When she calls out a level, take a listen and write it down. Her calls are phenomenal. Thanks Angie.

❝Trade the Futures market but love trading with Stefanie. She and I see the market the same. If you just follow her calls you will stay on the right side of the market. No Thinking.❞

Angela

John, aka Jay the Trader, is one of those people you just connect with right away. He found me through an article in Stocks and Commodities magazine. He attended the Dallas MoneyShow with a pen in hand, asking if I would sign his magazine. From that moment, Jay has dedicated himself to learning all my rules of trading. He carries around a book of all teachings like a trading bible. He now helps us out at our booth at all the shows. He also uses his air traffic controlling powers to make our flights get in early. Thank you, Jay, for all your help and support. We love you!

After several years of frustration in the market, I was ready to close all my trading accounts. Then I came across the article, "A Chat with Stefanie Kammerman" in the October 2016 issue of Stocks and Commodities Magazine.

It opened a door to a new trading approach which is simplified and consistently accurate. Since taking the Stock Whisperer's Boot Camp class, I have turned my accounts profitable. Thank you for your expertise in increasing my trading skills. A wise man once said, "The instruction you are willing to follow determines your salary." You are not only a first-class trader but an exceptional educator.

John Famularo (jaythetrader)

Gerald N is from Minnesota. He is one of our most consistent traders in the Pit. It has been a pleasure having him in our room sharing his trades with us. He's always following the whispers. Shhhhhhhhhhhhhhhhh...

What do I think about the Java Pit? It is a rare jewel in the field of investing.

Gerald N

Marie, aka Pinky Panther, from Toronto, is one of our most experienced traders in the room. She is one of the sweetest people out there, but she only gives her heart to people who deserve it. She will admit to stalking me for over a year before coming into our trading room. She will be the first to tell you that it is the best room out there. We shared some great memories cruising to Alaska. Her husband Mike is a great singer and a sweetheart too. We are so blessed to have these two in our family.

In 1968 I was taking a lunch break at my desk when one of the owners of the company walked by and asked what I was doing. I was looking up stock prices in the newspaper and with my pencil, ruler & graph paper adding the prices to my stock charts. He later hired me to work for him personally, managing his $20 million foundation portfolio. I did not make the buy/sell decisions, but I executed them for him. That involved writing a cheque and delivering it to the broker if it was a buy or going to the safety deposit box and extracting the paper stock certificate and delivering to the broker if it was a sell. When he passed away, I moved on to another career in publishing, then raising children and working in the cosmetics business.

Throughout those years, while I still loved to read the financial news and watch the stock market, I had no time to dedicate to it. Once my kids were educated and off on their own, I had a little more time to watch my nest egg building up. I had to retire at 50 due to my poor health and then after putting myself on a program for a few years to get healthier, I found I had more time and the desire to learn. Different interests caught my eye, but it was the stock market that drew me back.

Previously, I had signed up for the first online trading program that was available in Canada and put my investments there to manage. I took courses, attended seminars, and at one of these seminars, I heard Stefanie Kammerman speak for the first time. She was clearly a standout from all the other speakers. She impressed me with her sincerity, her knowledge of trading and her credibility. But I was of the ilk of those who believed in researching and finding great companies with increasing dividends, buying and holding them. I was beginning to swing trade more but I was not a short term trader.

certainly not a day trader and am still working to master options. It is just plain productive fun and I am grateful to Stefanie, Matthew and the trading group for enriching my life.

Pinky Panther (the name that Stef & Matt gave me the first time I was the Trader of the Day)"

Lorraine, aka Bird Lady, is from Colorado Springs. We call her the bird lady because she loves birds as much as she loves to trade. Lorraine and I share a special spiritual connection. Thank you for all those special emails Lorraine.

"I am a member of the Stock Whisperer trading room with Stefanie and I can say with conviction that it is THE best trading room out there! Stefanie has the experience and knowledge of how to master the markets! I have taken courses before but I have learned so much more from Stefanie! She discusses points I have not heard others talk about but are so key to making money!

The prints are really the way to enhancing your success in a trade especially when used in conjunction with the charts. As Stef says, "No thinking... bullish above, bearish below" the price level of the print- this has really enhanced my ability to make money in the markets.

Not only is Stefanie great at what she does but I really like her sincerity, warmth and candor. She is very genuine and really cares about people- something you do not see on Wall Street.

With all the insider trading and manipulation on Wall Street, this really helps the "little guy" to get an idea what the big boys are doing.

Really love this chat room and Stefanie!

Sincerely,
Lorraine B

John E, aka Block Head, from Michigan, always has my back. He has helped me make money, saved me a lot of money, corrected me numerous times, and always knows all the prints. He is also on top of all the stock news. He is the man who told us years ago about the block trade indicator. This indicator has changed our lives. We will forever be grateful to you John for that, as well as all that you have shared with us in our trading room.

The Java Pit is a great place to meet other traders, to learn from them and to gain inspiration from their success.

John E

 **Chad C** is a trader from Wisconsin. We met Chad at the Vegas show after he watched me during the live trading challenge. We enjoyed quite a few dinners together in Vegas and look forward to a lot more. He also helps us out at our booth as the third bald guy when he is in town. Thanks Chad!

I had been trading fairly successfully since 1995, but that all changed in 2014 when I met Stefanie. We met on accident as I was in Vegas to see an acquaintance in a live trading competition, his opponent was Stef. I was immediately drawn to some of the items she talked about during the competition, so much so that I decided to take in her presentation later in the day. It turned out to be one of the best decisions I have ever made. I joined her room the following week and never looked back.

I watched and listened to Stefanie for a couple months. I then combined her rules and techniques with my already successful trading plan and the results proved to be nothing short of phenomenal. The ability to listen to her each morning, as well as interact with her throughout the day is a tremendous benefit. I would be remiss to not mention the wonderful traders in the Java Pit, many of whom offer knowledge, ideas, techniques and inspiration. Someday I hope to have more time in my schedule so I can give back the way they have.

I highly recommend Stefanie and the Java Pit to everyone, from beginning traders to advanced traders, there is something there for everyone.

Chad C

Karl, aka Santa, from Toronto, does really look like Santa Claus. One of the first things Karl noticed about me was my painted blue toenails. He stuck around to learn everything I could teach him about trading around the Dark Pool. He has given us a gift back by doing numerous presentations in our room of candlesticks and how to use TC2000 to set up the best scans.

I started investing in 1996 reading every book I could get my hands on, watching seminars and attempting to train myself. I found this was a hit and miss method at best! In the year 2013 is when I listened in on a chat line and became interested in Stefanie's style of training.

I find her method of teaching is the way my mind works using charts, levels, moving averages and more to build a strong foundation upon which to trade. I have no regrets, my intentions are to continue my membership with The Stock Whisper and enjoying the "trading room" where we work as a team. I will continue building my knowledge creating a strong foundation upon which to trade.

knowledge is power.

Education is extremely essential when trading, swing trading or investing. it is important to avoid wishing, hoping or best guess."

Karl

Lil, aka Miss Sniper, from South Carolina, has put a lot of spunk into our trading room over the years. She has been an exceptional student who calls out great trades. She earned her nickname during our trading challenge in Boot Camp. It has been such a pleasure getting to know you Lil. I know many of the women in the room have also loved getting to know you as well.

"*I found Stef purely be accident and boy am I glad I did. The Java Pit has been a great experience for me. All of the members are very supportive and Stef is a born teacher with endless patience. In my quest to learn to become a better trader. I found exactly what I was looking for. a tried and true method that once learned. can be used without having to rely on someone else's trading software.*"

Lil

Neil, aka Mr. Diamond is from California. Neil speaks his mind. His great idea for WOW, Women of Wealth, has been a successful implementation at the TradersEXPO and the MoneyShow conventions. We have enjoyed so many amazing apple martinis and dinners together with him and his wife Jodi. We look forward to cruising to Italy with them on the Stock Whisperers Trading Cruise.

Jake B, aka The Swinger, is from North Bay, Ontario. Jake and I go way back together. Over the years we have made many nickel bets on so many things. When we finally got to meet each other, I had to bring a lot of nickels with me. Jake is the luckiest man. His beautiful wife Krista is a sweetheart, an astute business woman, a wonderful mom, and a phenomenal cook. She was one of the wives that had to sit next to their husbands during my "Finding the T-Spot" workshop. I guess it wasn't too bad. Jake has stuck around for many years, and Krista is no longer suspicious of me. He is a lifetime member of the Pit.

After the crash of 2000, I decided to take a more active role in my investments and took my advisor to task on all their mutual fund recommendations. Things were going 'ok' until 2008 when another crash occurred and once again I cringed when I looked at my portfolio. Fifteen years of investing and nothing to show for it. The old buy and hold, average down methods were not working. It was then I decided that no one cares about my money as I do, and I became a self-directed investor. I read every investing book I could get my hands on and subscribed to numerous advisories. But my results were mediocre. Something was missing. I needed a mentor. I paid several popular investing gurus but they just gave me handouts, a few verbal lessons, and sent me out on my own. I was lost.

Then, in 2011, I met Stefanie Kammerman. She had a different approach. She taught trading courses online, from beginner to master, and she provided direct one-on-one coaching. She gave me personal access to ask any question, anytime, and responded with detailed lessons. But more than that, she is with me and the other traders every day in an online trading room, during live market hours, providing instant advice, guidance, and impromptu trading lessons applicable to the market at that very moment, as well as sharing trading ideas. Stefanie taught me day and swing trading, and more importantly the discipline and patience needed for such an emotionally demanding profession. And now? I day and swing trade with confidence, and even provide advice to others in the trading room. And I am happily profitable!! But the best thing about Stefanie? She cares about my trading, and my money, as much as I do.

Jake B

Kent C and his wife **Janet** are very special people. They are the kindest souls. They are from Vancouver. Kent is a phenomenal painter with a brilliant mind. We have enjoyed quite a few dinners together over the years. We have been trading together for a very long time.

Stef is the teacher that gave me the tools to start studying trading. I got much support from the wonderful group of people she has brought together in the Java Pit who also help me trade and learn about trading.

Kent

Bruce aka "The Brucinator" and his wife Laura, from Seattle, are the sweetest couple you will meet. I love when couples share the same passion for trading. It was fantastic having dinner with them and getting to meet them in person. It's been a fantastic experience for me to watch them grow as traders in the Pit.

Stefanie Kammerman is the most friendly, approachable, and experienced trading coach we have ever had. My wife and I have been in other trading rooms that charge WAY too much money and have very subjective rules for their trading plan. Stef is different – she is definitive with her rules – and her rules bring results. Results that feel calculated and expected - not accidental or lucky.

Stef specializes in following the smart money, specifically big Dark Pool prints. She says first comes the prints, then comes the news, then comes the move - prints always come first. She teaches you how to read the prints and what to do about it.

For example, on June 7, 2017, we made a trade in BABA before the close of the day because there was a huge Dark Pool print. The next morning we closed it out and made over 1966% ROI on the trade! THAT is real results.

Of course, we wished we would have met Stef a long time ago, but we are with her now and have never been happier. Thanks for everything, Stef!"

Bruce Linker and Laura Geres

William C, from Dallas, Texas, sat quietly for a long time observing if I was the real deal or not. He stalked me until he felt comfortable to let me know how much money he has made off what I teach in the Pit. He told me that once he trusts and respects somebody, that you have him for life. William has given me some phenomenal advice when I first announced I was going to write this book. I thank you for that Bill. He has an amazing son-in-law named Ben who is also a phenomenal trader.

> *I am a 30+ year trader. I have learned more under Stefanie than the last 30 years combined. As I am getting 4 crossing 8 alerts, I owe it all to her! I have been in the room and taking her mentoring for a little over a year now. The results have been astounding! I simply don't know how I made any money before!*
>
> *Stefanie is the hardest working and most generous person I know - with a huge heart! She deserves all the success and happiness there is - She's earned it!*
>
> *Bill C*

Christopher S, from Norfolk, Virginia, found me through a Lightspeed™ presentation I did on the Dark Pool. Within his first month of being in the Pit, he has had amazing success. He is a natural at this. There aren't too many traders that pick this up so quickly, but he has proven that he has.

Blanca, from Mississauga, Ontario, is one of my favorite students. She is one of the most disciplined and conservative traders that I have met. I get the most joy as a teacher when I have students like Blanca. She calls out great stuff all day long. Her eagerness to learn will give her tremendous success in the future. I love having her in the Java Pit and enjoy trading with her every day.

I was 16 years old when I had my first experience with markets. I walked my mother to a gold dealer where she borrowed US dollars against her gold jewelry. That is when I learned the value of gold. After many years, I decided to pursue a degree in Business and ended up working in accounting, but the idea of becoming a stock trader was always there. I decided to do some trading on my own and made $250 CAD on my first trade but lost $2000 right after (traded a biotechnology stock); I got scared, depressed and quit for a while until I found Stef through Larry Berman's website. I downloaded her workshop called "Counting the Cards of Wall Street" and took notes like crazy that night, it was then when I had my first "aha" moment. However, the real hands-on trading experience started when I took Stefanie's Boot Camp class. It was eyes opening for me. I learned about rules, levels and techniques for trading.

Almost everyone in my family did not support my decision except my husband, since they thought there is no way someone on the internet can teach you how to trade and that only the big banks can make profits, but that did not stop me because I knew that Stefanie was a profitable trader (she trades live on the Java Pit by calling out her entries and exits) and I could learn from her and was willing to work very hard for it.

One of the many advantages of being at the Java Pit is presence of other successful traders who I respect and

> *admire for their valuable teachings but most of all, is the non-stoppable coaching of Stefanie for which I am deeply grateful.*
>
> *Blanca*

 **Jan L.** from Ontario. It was such a pleasure to finally meet Jan at the Toronto MoneyShow. We had such a great dinner together with the other traders from the Java Pit. Jan and I have many things in common. Motherhood and trading are just two of them. She has been a wonderful student and the progress she has made has been exceptional.

> *I used to have my money handled by a financial advisor. It drove me crazy how much I was paying in commissions and my portfolio wasn't increasing. A very successful friend of mine told me to move my money into a self-directed account and he would help me with my investments (for free!). I started following stocks on StockTwits and was so fascinated by it all. I wanted to learn more. Over the next 4 years, I took 4 boot camps with 4 different people. All different styles but none of them made me a successful trader. I realized that I didn't want to be a "follower"... I wanted to really understand the trades. I lost a lot of money during those 4 years but I learned a lot. As they say... you learn from your mistakes. I found Stefanie on StockTwits. I followed along with her "Whisper of the Day"*

and saw how consistent she was. I joined her chat room and quickly realized that I needed to take her boot camp. I took her boot camp 1 year ago. What I learned from her was life changing. Following the prints works.

Stefanie has taught me how to follow the prints. I can now trade on my own and I don't have to "follow" anyone. I wish I would have met Stefanie 4 years ago when I started trading. It would have saved me a lot of money. She is a great teacher... as well as a very caring person. Even though she is trading herself all day long, she will always take the time to answer questions and to explain things. She comes on the microphone twice a day and I write down everything she says. Every day, she gives someone the title of "Trader of the Day". I have received this award a couple of times now and it truly is an honour to be recognized by her!! I will never leave her trading room since I learn from her every single day. She is truly AMAZING!!!

Jan L

Stevan, aka Mr. Sinatra Singer, is from Utah. Not only is he a phenomenal trader, he performs at retirement homes by singing Sinatra hits to the elderly. He is another angel on this earth. I had the pleasure of cruising to Alaska with him and his wife Leuri. Not all our traders who come into our room are beginners. Traders like Stevan, who are advanced, come into our room and add so much by calling out great trades consistently.

Since joining the Java Pit and The Stock Whisperer with Stefanie Kammerman just a few months ago, my trading success has exploded to the upside. I've traded for over 30 years, yet now I trade with new confidence that I'm on the right side of the market, long or short, stocks or options, or both. Over and over again, after identifying prints in the Dark Pool and taking a position, the market moves in my direction like it was controlled by some outside force. The experience is enhanced further as Stefanie personally calls the market live during trading hours, discloses her own trades, cheers on the traders in the trading room (Java Pit), and even admits when she makes mistakes (which is rare, but any trader who claims they don't is lying). Every morning I can't wait to get to my trading room because I'm confident I'm going to make money, and I get excited because we have fun supporting each other in the process. Maybe I'm new to The Stock Whisperer, but seventeen out of nineteen winning trades is hard to ignore, so I plan to be around for awhile. Thank you Stefanie and your team, for putting together the best trading experience of my career.

You are the real deal; a truly remarkable human being, and I'm honored and thrilled to have made your acquaintance.

Stevan R Davis,"Mr. Sinatra Singer"

Paul, aka The Alien, who lives in Sacramento, was courageous enough to sit in the front row during my presentation in that city. Front row attendees typically are the only ones to join the Java Pit, so I knew he would be the most likely candidate to join our trading room. I love how eager he has been to learn how to trade the Dark Pool. I knew right away that he'd be one of my best students.

In the Java Pit, there are plenty of suggestions and observations from the other members who spot stocks, ETF's and other instruments which are moving or about to move with momentum. Add to that, the Dark Pool block trades, shown in real time on the screen gives me an edge to know when a stock is about to move up or down and helps immensely with entry and exit points. I use the pit to complement my trading plan and work it around my day. I use the Java Pit for a few day trades but mostly for swing trading which is more my style. It helps make my trading, more precise, less lonely and more interactive and thus much more enjoyable. It helps keep me honest and cuts down the number of mistakes I make by getting feedback on potential trades. Overall I would say it is an excellent community of positive traders from all walks of life. I recommend you check it out and see if it might help you.

Paul, The Alien

 **Jim D, aka Mr. Fibonacci**, runs the biggest and best traders meetup group in New York called The Long Island Stock Traders Meetup Group. His group has regular monthly meetings at the Plainview Library. Jim has done many amazing presentations on how to use Fibonacci retracements and extensions. He has many fantastic calls on where the market is headed. His wife Elaine is a sweetheart. You're a lucky man Jim.

> *There are diverse types of trading, but you need to start with a foundation. The experience I've had with Stefanie's Java Pit is second to none to obtain that foundation. The Java Pit gives the insight on how to find stocks, whether you're a day trader, swing trader or even as an investor. It helped me to understand the innovative ways to trade the Dark Pool for more profit. Her presentations at our Stock Traders Meetup Group has been overwhelmingly welcomed by the members. I've known Stefanie for the past eight years and I have learned to respect the ability and good sense she has brought to the investment community. This book is a testimony to her achievements.*
>
> *James De Franco*
> *Organizer, Long Island Stock Traders Meetup Group*

 **Andrew L**, from Reno Nevada,

I was just going to let you know you said something yesterday and it probably snuck right past most people. You said you have to master yourself not the market. That is a priceless statement and I hope you continue to say it. Trading with you taught me how to master myself. Obviously having a system that works helps but you and your personality helped push me over the edge. In a good way of course lol. Thank you so much, these Dark Pool prints make trading very simple and low stress as well as very profitable with very low risk.

Thank You Again,
Andy

Kody A, aka Sharkman is one of our favorite traders in the pit. Not only does he trade like a shark, but his services in the military are commendable. With two deployments in Iraq, as well working as a medic in Afghanistan, we thank you Kody for all your services and we are honored to have you as a Pitter.

I have been in many trading chat rooms but, The Java Pit is by far my favorite room to be part of. Stefanie is always willing to answer your questions, evaluate your trades and help make you a better trader. If Stefanie is busy assisting other traders, there is always another member that is eager to point you to the right direction. Since learning how to trade around the Dark Pool by Stefanie Kammerman, my success rate has definitely increased. Thank you, Stef, for teaching me to swim with the sharks in the Dark Pool.

Kody A

Jim and Andrea are the loveliest couple who opened their Utah home to me on my birthday. They prepared the most delicious home-cooked vegan meal just for me. They even went out of their way to find the best vegan chocolate cake out there. Thank you for your amazing hospitality. What a great birthday gift!

Japhy G, aka Datatraderpro, is from Toronto. We immediately became friends when we both found out that we were obsessed with the Dark Pool. He created software to track Dark Pool data, initially for himself because he found it difficult to get the data in Canada. He now shares Dark Pool data with traders all over the world through his website. He provides market internals using bubble graphs, along with many other tools for traders. Thank you Data for helping us traders out.

Sarah B found us through StockTwits:

"I am new to the Java Pit trading room. I will admit that I hesitated to join the Java Pit for two reasons: 1) I really wasn't interested in following someone else's buy and sell signals. 2) I had very little experience in trading rooms and wasn't sure I'd get anything out of it, except more noise during the trading day. Wow, was I wrong on both counts! I learned more about the stock market and options in my first month, than I did in two years (thousands of dollars spent) of educational courses. I'm not saying the money I spent on my education was wasted, far from it; however, when you trade for a living or even trade as a hobby, you quickly figure out that the trading game is not played on a level playing field. For me, The Java Pit helps to level the playing field. Stefanie (the Stock Whisperer) is a fantastic trader and educator and she has other Pro traders in the room as well. They all encourage and support trading with your own trading plan, not just following someone else's trades. I was so intrigued from my first day in the room, that I did something I swore I'd never do. I spent more money on one of Stefanie's Options courses. I did not regret it. In fact, I've already improved my trading and I've modified my own trading plan based on what I learned in the course. I completely recovered the money spent on the course in two trades. I am very excited to have found the Java Pit trading room and excited about my future as a full time trader. My sincere thanks to the Stock Whisperer and all the other traders in the Java Pit."

Sarah B

I saved the best for last: **Matthew, aka Matt Support**. Matthew does the job of at least nine people. He is both my management and administration teams. He is my producer on all my videos. He is my stage manager and director at live presentations. He provides customer support and technical support. He does the in-house accounting. He is my PowerPoint designer and my wardrobe coordinator. He is my travel agent. He is my equipment manager when we travel. And he does hundreds of other tasks as they come up. He is the man behind the scenes that makes all the magic happen. He is everybody's best friend. Thank you for everything that you do Matthew. I, as well as everyone in the Java Pit, love you!

We must also give an honorable mention to our Newbie traders who have recently come into our trading room and our Old Timers who have been around for many years.

Pitters that have passed: Our angels in heaven

Sean, aka the red-haired step child, was a special angel. Sean always made us laugh. He was a Canadian who loved to trade gold and copper so much he would joke about painting his toenails in metallic colors. We would always ask him what color his toenails were for that day. He seemed to be able to move the metals depending upon the different colors. Sean would always pick me up from the airport when I presented in Vancouver, armed with homemade sandwiches and a bottle of wine. He stuck up for me when Larry Berman heckled me during my first presentation in Vancouver. Not a day goes by in the Java Pit that we don't miss him. May you rest in peace Sean.

Roy Sangster was a very kind man and a great friend who was too young to go. He is missed.

NOTES:

NOTES:

NOTES:

NOTES:

NOTES:

NOTES:

NOTES:

NOTES:

NOTES: